FEMINISM and PROCESS THOUGHT

THE HARVARD DIVINITY SCHOOL/CLAREMONT CENTER FOR PROCESS STUDIES SYMPOSIUM PAPERS

Edited by
SHEILA GREEVE DAVANEY

D1547738

THE EDWIN MELLEN PRESS
NEW YORK AND TORONTO

For Information
The Edwin Mellen Press
P.O. Box 450
Lewiston, NY 14092

Symposium Series, Volume Six

ISBN 0-88946-903-2

Symposium Series ISBN 0-88946-989-X

Library of Congress Catologing Number 81-3942

Printed in the United States of America

TABLE OF CONTENTS

INTRODUCTION

SHEILA GREEVE DAVANEY

The essays in this volume originated at the Conference on Feminism and Process Thought sponsored by Harvard Divinity School and the Center for Process Studies in Claremont, California.[1] Individual women and men had been reflecting for some time upon the often common issues raised by each of these perspectives and upon the possibility of exchange and conversation between the two schools of thought. But, for the most part, these efforts had been isolated and scattered, lacking the opportunity for enrichment and development that emerges from dialogue. The Conference on Feminism and Process Thought represented the first formal attempt to remedy this situation. The overall purpose of the conference was to provide a context within which proponents of feminism and process thought could explore areas of convergence and divergence both in relation to the fundamental assertions of the perspective of each and in terms of the material and concrete repercussions of these principles. The essays offered herein are the first, but presumably not last, fruits of this conversation.

Interchange between feminism and process thought is significant because both make common assertions and share fundamental presuppositions. Both thoroughly reject traditional Western ways of conceiving of self, world, and God.[2] Both assert that Western humanity has primarily understood

the world dualistically and patterned reality hierarchically.
Being, within this traditional vision, has been elevated over
becoming, static over dynamic activity, independence and
self-completeness over interdependence and relatedness. Furthermore, primary differentiations have been made between God
and the world, men and women, humanity and nature. In each
instance, one side of the dualistic model has been understood
as subject, with intrinsic value and power, while the other
has been an object valued solely in relation to the subject.
In each instance, the first term has defined the identity and
value of the second.

Proponents of feminism and process thought see this dualistic and hierarchical vision of reality as existentially
and intellectually inadequate.   Many feminists trace this
conception of reality to what we consider the oldest and most
fundamental dualism -- the hierarchical differentiation between women and men. And all feminists see in this hierarchical differentiation, whatever its historical origin, continued justification for our oppression. Analogously, adherents of process thought see the inadequacy of this hierarchical interpretation of reality in numerous ways; it coheres
poorly with the presuppositions of an age circumscribed by
the claims of modern science, of quantum theory and relativity physics; it counters many contemporary assertions of
sociology, political theory, and psychology; perhaps most
importantly, it fails to respond adequately to the existential concerns of our era, to questions of order and value in
a century fragmented by world conflict, continued oppression,
the threat of ecological disaster and the prospect of final
global destruction.

Thus adherents of feminism and process thought advocate
rejecting views of reality primarily and profoundly characteristic of Western life for much of the last twenty centuries. But this is the negative description of the ground
shared by feminism and process thought. Stated positively,
both perspectives are primarily concerned with developing a

wholistic, rather than a dualistic, understanding of reality.
To develop such an organic model, both perspectives begin by
affirming the essential subjectivity of all that exists. And
both suggest that this subjectivity is essentially social,
creative and processive. Here is a brief description of the
way both feminism and process thought interpret this subjectivity.

Feminist thinker Mary Daly, for example, states that
"to exist humanly is to name the self, the world and God."[4]
Most feminists agree with Daly's assertion that women have
been oppressed on the most fundamental level because we have
been denied this power of naming which has consequently excluded us from creating our own identities. Interpretations
of reality emerge from and reflect their social contexts.
But unlike most men, women have been denied significant participation in this meaning process. Yet we have nonetheless
been forced to live our lives in terms of visions we did not
create. Women are presently reclaiming our right to self-
definition and, indeed, our right to contribute to the definition of reality itself. Women are now establishing our
identity as women, finding our value first and foremost in
ourselves, not solely from our connection with men. Women
are now claiming that each of us is a subject who must be
understood as being someone for herself.

The vision of reality developed by Alfred North
Whitehead and proponents of the process school of thought
offers a metaphysical system based upon an understanding of the
self consistent with women's emerging reflections upon our experience.[5] For Whitehead all our conceptualizations must
start with experiencing subjects. Whitehead understands
these experiencing subjects as units or momentary instances
of process and analyzes them under two broad aspects -- as
subjects for themselves in the immediacy of their own experience and as objects available to contribute to subsequent experiencing subjects.

Whitehead explores the first aspect of subjectivity in
terms of concrescence or the process of becoming. A subject
understood from the perspective of concrescence is the merging of
elements of the past world into the unity of a unique and novel
present. Several important points should be noted here. First,
this subject must be understood as intrinsically social or
relational. Each moment of becoming relates internally to the
given past world. Every subject must consider what has already occurred. In this sense dependence is intrinsic to
subjectivity. Each subject is a product of its history.

Secondly, and equally important, fundamental freedom is
intrinsic to any subject, to any instance of becoming. Existence necessarily entails freedom. Because every subject is
the product of its past no such thing as absolute, uncondi-
tional freedom exists. Yet no subject is totally determined
by its past. Every subject plays a self-determining role in
its own creation. Although each subject emerges from its past,
it is self-creative in relation to it. Hence, within the process perspective, the interpretation of reality begins with
the experiencing subject, understood as essentially valuable in
and for itself and as exhibiting simulataneously the characteristics of freedom and social determination.

These process notions of dependence, freedom, and the
intrinsic value of the experiencing subject offer a conceptual
apparatus appropriate to feminist experience. The process
perspective reflects and affirms the feminist understanding
of women as subjects. It also offers a context in which to
see our relation to the past and to our world as embodying
both value and freedom. It corresponds to our experiential
recognition of ourselves as self-created centers of experience and supports our realization that we participate in our
own self-creation without being limited to externally determined definitions.

But an affirmation of ourselves as subjects involves as
well the recognition that we contribute to the experience of

others. Now women are wary of any definition of women that
includes the idea of women as objects because history has
portrayed us almost exclusively in these terms. Nonetheless,
we insist that understanding women as individual and unique
subjects does not exclude our recognition that we also contribute to others. With our recognition that we are subjects
comes our awareness that not only are we values for ourselves
but for others as well.

Within the process perspective this assertion also is
fundamental to understanding subjectivity. A subject is not
just something in and for itself. For Whitehead, an instance
of becoming endures but a moment, reaches completion, and by
so doing becomes available to contribute to the world of suc-
ceeding experiencing subject. As a unit of process reaches
completion it then becomes part of the fixed, determined and
determining past which then must be taken account of by subsequent concrescing subjects. If a subject must be conceived
as a value in the immediacy of its own becoming, it must
equally well be understood as a value to be appropriated by
others.

Thus within the feminist and process perspectives all
entities have value both in themselves and for others. But,
most importantly, this value *for* others rests upon the positive intrinsic value of the experiencing subject. All entities contribute to units of experience beyond themselves,
but no entity can be an object which is not first a subject.

Both feminism and process thought affirm a vision of
reality based on the essential subjectivity of all that exists.
Both affirm a world full of intrinsically valuable and self-
creative subjects. Both recognize the importance of the past
and affirm the possibility of creative contribution to the
future. Hence, their fundamental presuppositions and their
common rejection of traditional interpretations of reality,

provides feminism and process thought substantial grounds for
colloboration.

Other reasons also make this collaboration fruitful.
Much feminist thought, especially theological reflection, has
to date, opposed prevalent conceptions of self, world, and
God. Increasingly, however, feminist thinkers are directing
attention away from this essentially negative activity toward constructing alternative views. Process thought, with
its highly developed metaphysical vision, may well provide a
conceptual framework to explain and relate the experience of
women to the rest of reality.

Similarly, feminism and the experience of women can contribute much to process thought. Although process thought
has criticized traditional conceptions, it has ignored femal
experience. Like its conceptual opponents, it has been primarily a male construction. Women can contribute in a uniqu
two-fold manner to process thought. First, our experience
can test the applicability of process categories: through an
alyzing female experience we can judge how well the broad
metaphysical categories of process thought reflect and express particular concrete experience. Second, such analysi
of women's experience can creatively further the development
of process thinking. Because the female dimension of experi
ence has not previously been addressed by process thinkers,
its inclusion will enlarge this philosophical movement.

The essays in this volume reflect, develop, and deepen
the themes suggested above. They all exhibit similar ap-
proaches and continously echo common concerns. Their contin
uity can be seen in each author's beginning with an autobio-
graphical explication of how feminism and process thought in
teract. Such a procedure mirrors the authors' commonly held
conviction that "personalizing" conceptual activity enhances
rather than diminishes, the integrity of the intellectual
endeavor.

This continuity also appears in each thinker's approach to feminism and process thought. Each examines a profound problem feminism and the experience of women highlights. Some of these problems have been perennial difficulties emerging in every age. Others have only emerged fully with our own times. All, articulated and analyzed from the perspective of female experience, assume uniqueness and new urgency. Valerie Saiving, John Cobb, Penelope Washbourn, and Marjorie Suchocki all examine a set of dualisms constitutive of the traditional model of reality. They then explore ways such seemingly antithetical pairs might be more creatively re-interpreted through process categories and the insights of female experience. Saiving explores the traditional dualism of individuality and relatedness; Cobb examines the relation of the body to the "soul" or self; Washbourn investigates the connection between distinctive bodily experience and female sexuality, and the definition of what it means to be a woman; Suchocki looks anew at the perennial problem of the relationship between God and the world; and finally, Jean Lambert, in the concluding essay, applies feminist and process perspectives to the concrete and complicated ethical dilemma of abortion.

The essays range from complex theoretical discussions to concrete difficulties of decision making. In all cases, these thinkers assert that examining these problems reveals underlying metaphysical difficulties; consequently, these problems cannot be resolved by mere shifts within traditional ways of of conceiving of reality. Any truly adequate resolution demands a fundamentally altered view of reality. Indeed, a commonly held conviction of these thinkers is that our present problematic way of conceiving these problems reflects a dualistic and hierarchical world view. Finally, all these thinkers propose that the combined insights of feminism and process thought may offer new and creative ways for reevaluating these problems.

I want to acknowledge and thank those who made the conference and this subsequent publication possible. Dr. John
Cobb has been the primary source of encouragement for this
project. Without his support it would never have taken
place. The Center for Process Studies, a co-sponsor of the
conference, and its staff, particularly David Vergin, have
provided both financial assistance and generous clerical
help.

Harvard Divinity School is the second sponsor of the
conference, and members of the Divinity School community were
actively involved in planning the event. The coordinators o:
Women's Programs, Brinton Lykes and Constance Buchanan, offered organizational expertise and helpful personal support.
Dean Krister Stendahl not only provided financial support,
and linked the conference with the Dudelian Lectureship for
the year, he also created an atmosphere conducive to fruitfu
and lively interchange. The Harvard Divinity School Theolog
Department made further contributions. Moreover, the confer
ence was carried out by all the members of the Committee on
Feminism and Process Thought: Brinton Lykes, Ruth Smith, and
Paula Cooey-Nichols.

I am especially grateful to those who presented conference papers. Their efforts contributed greatly to the conversation between feminism and process thought. They have,
hope, laid the foundation for continued development in this
area. I also wish to thank all the conference and workshop
participants. Many came from as far away as California,
Canada, and West Virginia. Their enthusiasm testified to th
worth of the project; their energy and participation made th
conference a success.

Finally I want to thank Professor Herbert Richardson o:
The Edwin Mellen Press who saw in these essays ideas worthy

of publication and helped make them available to a wider
audience.

Cambridge, Massachusetts
1981

NOTES

[1]The conference took place at Harvard University in
autumn, 1978. The essays by Valerie Saiving, John Cobb, and
Marjorie Suchocki are essentially the same as presented at
the conference. Penelope Washbourn's essay is an expanded
version of her conference paper. Jean Lambert, a respondent
at the conference, has included an entirely new essay for
this volume. Mary Daly, who delivered a paper at the conference, chose not to include it in this volume but to include
it in her *Gyn/Ecology* (Boston: Beacon Press, 1979).

[2]It would be impossible, and perhaps even undesirable,
to speak for *all* feminists or process thinkers. Hence it
should be recognized that these comments represent only one
person's interpretation of feminism and process thought.
Nonetheless, I think that the interpretation suggested here
is in substantial agreement with the views set forth in the
following essays. Furthermore, although not speaking for all
women, I have used the first person pronouns in order to
self-consciously acknowledge the perspective from which these
remarks are made.

[3]The proponents of feminism and process thought alike
recognize that throughout the history of Western thought and
life there have been many deviations and variations of what
is here called the traditional world view. Nonetheless, in
general terms, dualism and hierarchy have been the salient
characteristics which have prevailed in the context of
Western thinking.

[4]Mary Daly, *Beyond God the Father: Toward a Philosophy of Women's Liberation* (Boston: Beacon Press, 1973) 8.

[5]This introduction and the other essays in this volume deal with process thought most often with reference to Alfred North Whitehead. This is because Whitehead is considered the founder of the process school of thought and it is he who developed the most thorough and complete metaphysical articulation of process claims. However it should be noted that prior to Whitehead a number of thinkers developed their own positions in somewhat analogous ways to Whitehead (among them Hegel and Bergson) and that many of Whitehead's followers have presented substantial positions of their own (most notably Charles Hartshorne). Hence, although the dialogue pursued herein has looked to Whitehead, there are other directions open for exploration as well.

ANDROGYNOUS LIFE:

A FEMINIST APPROPRIATION OF PROCESS THOUGHT

(THE HARVARD UNIVERSITY DUDELIAN LECTURE)

VALERIE C. SAIVING

It is appropriate that the Dudelian Lecture on Natural
Religion be devoted to the mutual relevance of feminism and
process philosophy, for these two modes of thought agree, in
Whitehead's words, that "we can only deal with things in some
sense experienced";[1] both insist that all constructive
thought has "its origin in the generalization of particular
factors discerned in particular topics of human interest";[2]
and each "refuses to place human experience outside nature."[3]
Feminists and process thinkers also agree that what counts as
"experience" has been far too narrowly defined in traditional
philosophy -- that if metaphysical inquiry begins in "subjective experiencing,"[4] it is essential that *every variety*
of experience be taken into account:

> experience drunk and experience sober, experience
> sleeping and experience waking, experience drowsy
> and experience wide-awake, experience self-conscious
> and experience self-forgetful, experience intel-
> lectual and experience physical, experience religi-
> ous and experience skeptical, experience anxious and
> experience carefree, experience anticipatory and ex-
> perience retrospective, experience happy and experi-
> ence grieving, experience dominated by emotions and
> experience under self-restraint, experience in the

light and experience in the dark, experience normal
and experience abnormal.[5]

To which feminists now emphatically add: experience female
and experience male.

I speak as both a feminist and a Whiteheadian. A brief
account of how I arrived at this combined perspective may
throw some light on what I have to say.

As a graduate student in theology in the mid-nineteen
forties, I was absorbed in the study of process philosophy.
At that time, I did not think of myself as a feminist, although I now see that in some ways I was living as though the
feminist dream of androgynous life were about to come true.
But for the next decade or so I abandoned my study of Whitehead
for *Better Homes and Gardens*. During those years I was trying
to be a "complete woman," as our culture defined womanhood.
In the late fifties, however, a series of events in my personal life awoke in me the first stirrings of feminist consciousness. At the same time I resumed my theological
studies. At first these two changes in my life were connected
only in an external way: my desire to teach, suddenly freed
by a sense of the possibilities now open to me, made it important to complete my graduate work. But it soon became
apparent that there was a deeper connection: as I tried to
understand the transformation I had experienced, I discovered
that process philosophy provided the conceptual framework I
needed. Although this framework had been there all along, I
had suppressed it, because the androgynous vision embodied in
Whitehead's philosophy was fundamentally incompatible with
the non-androgynous ideal around which I had been trying to
shape my life.

From this personal history I draw two conclusions relevant to any exploration of the relations between feminism and
process thought. On the one hand, not even an intimate ac-
quaintance with Whitehead's ideas is capable of *creating* feminist consciousness; such consciousness arises out of certain

kinds of life experience, explored in dialogue with other
women. On the other hand, feminist consciousness, once
awakened, seeks a conceptual framework for self-understanding,
and process philosophy may provide such a framework.

This does not mean, in Mary Daly's words, that feminists
should let any "prefabricated theory have *authority* over us,"
for "The essential thing is to hear our *own* experience."[6]
This warning is completely consistent with Whitehead's view
that the primary datum for metaphysics "is nothing else than
the experiencing subject,"[7] and that "In order to acquire
learning, we must first shake ourselves free of it."[8] Systematic thought is necessary, but we must not allow ourselves
to be seduced into the "dismissal of experience in the interest of system."[9]

But if Whitehead implicitly challenges women resolutely
to think out of our own experience, he also reminds us that
human experience never comes uninterpreted. At one level,
feminists already know this, for to be a feminist is to be
aware of the power of cultural images and theories of women
to twist our experiences and understanding of ourselves into
hurtful and hateful shapes. Yet even as we recognize this
fact and struggle to express what we really are and hope for,
we become aware that all thinking, including feminist thinking, takes place within a network of unconscious and semi-
conscious presuppositions about the wider context within
which *all* experience occurs. Ultimately, this network constitutes an implicit metaphysics whose premises are embedded
in our institutions, in the structure and lexicon of our
language, and in the unquestioned deliverances of "common
sense." These premises, although not obviously patriarchal,
nevertheless shape and are shaped by patriarchical structures
and modes of thought. So long as they remain unconscious,
they threaten to vitiate our attempts to understand and express our emerging vision. We must, then, bring more fully

into consciousness and criticize our unexamined notions about the nature of things. To do this is to engage in metaphysical inquiry.

Perhaps even now a wholly original metaphysics is being constructed on the basis of women's unique experience. But no such metaphysics has yet appeared, and I suspect that there is no Archimedean point at which to begin to create it. In any event, until it does appear, it seems reasonable for feminists to begin with some already existing philosophical scheme, building upon it, criticizing and correcting it, and reconstructing it where necessary in the light of our conversation with each other.

I name this process "feminist appropriation," borrowing a term used by Whitehead to suggest the *creative* way in which an occasion of experience responds to and uses the past from it own perspective and for its own purposes. Feminist appropriation of any philosophical system will be active, critical, and imaginative; it will be open to new ways of thinking but will take nothing on authority; and it will insist on testing every hypothesis by reference to the immediate experience of women.

Clearly, most philosophical systems are unsuitable candidates for feminist appropriation, either because they are explicitly sexist, or because they repel criticism based on *any* special form of experience. However, there are, I suggest, good reasons for thinking that Whitehead's metaphysics might be a creative alternative for appropriation by feminists. Besides the fact that, in principle, it invites a feminist critique, it is noteworthy that a number of feminists have found in Whitehead's writings observations which resonate with women's experience. Most important, however, Whitehead's metaphysics suggests ways of resolving certain problems within feminist thought, not by "indulg[ing] in brilliant feats of explaining away"[10] one or another of the

differing points of view, but by helping us to reconceptualize
the issues.

One such problem concerns the ideal of androgynous life.
For many feminists, androgynous life symbolizes the ultimate
goal of the women's movement. The ideal of androgyny begins
with the recognition that, out of the whole range of human
potentialities, certain traits have been differentially assigned to men and to women, and that all such systems of arbitrary distinctions between the sexes are crippling to
women (and ultimately to everyone). Androgyny is a form of
life in which every person will be enabled to become a whole
human being.

But the ideal of androgynous life is not without serious
difficulties from a feminist perspective. It has been observed, for instance, that the concept arises out of and
therefore is infected by the very assumption it is meant to
deny: namely, that certain characteristics are essentially
"feminine" and others essentially "masculine." While this
objection needs to be taken seriously, other objections are
even more basic. First, it is clear that some proponents of
the ideal have failed to recognize the *asymmetrical* relationship between the qualities traditionally ascribed to women a
and to men. "Femininity" is always defined as oriented to the
needs of men (and of children and society conceived as the
extensions of men's egos). "Masculinity," in contrast, is
never defined primarily as serving the needs of women. Another way of saying this is that the "masculine" is related
to the "feminine" in a pattern of dominance and subordination.
Given this pattern, the notion that women should acquire
"masculine" qualities in addition to their "feminine" traits,
and that men should develop their "feminine" side without
ceasing to be "masculine," is simply self-contradictory. If
masculinity involves domination over women and femininity
means subservience to men, then a man who developed his

"feminine" potentialities would no longer be masculine, and a woman who developed her "masculine" potentialities would cease to be feminine.

This objection to the ideal of androgyny can be carried a step further. Many feminists want nothing whatever to do with the "masculine" virtues. The qualities ascribed to men, especially in our culture -- qualities such as rationality, aggressiveness, objectivity, autonomy, competitiveness, ambition, even courage and boldness in action -- have been shaped by the pervasive context of domination. These qualities have therefore taken the form of exploiting and destroying women, other human beings, and our natural environment. Such "masculine" traits are not, from a feminist viewpoint, qualities to be admired in any human being, and they have no place in a feminist vision of the future.

Finally, we need to recognize that the ideal of androgyny has, up to now, been primarily a creation of the male intellect and, like every concept, bears the mark of its origin. When men envisage androgynous life, they do so from the perspective of their own position of actual or symbolic power over women. Thus, unconsciously, but most inevitably, they assume the continuation of their present powers, while imagining the acquisition of "feminine" qualities. No one has stated more incisively the assumptions which permeate the longings of some men for a more androgynous life than Simone de Beauvoir. "No man," she says, "would consent to be a woman, but every man wants women to exist";[11] and: "Man does not wish to be woman; but he dreams of *enfolding within him all that exists,* including therefore this woman, whom he is not."[12] Androgynous life, so conceived, is yet one more example of that imperialistic drive, inculcated as a "masculine" virtue in our society, to possess everything exclusively as one's own.[13] In this sense, the ideal of androgyny reinforces the status quo instead of providing a vision of liberation.

Still, feminist thinking cannot do without something
like the ideal of androgynous life. All feminists agree that
sexual stereotypes are false and damaging to women, and that
at least some of the qualities ascribed to men, and simultaneously forbidden to and punished in women, need to be fostered in all human beings: for example, the ability to discover who we are and what we want to be; the right to share
equally in making decisions which affect us all; the opportunity to develop all our capacities, mental, physical, spiritual; the right to find satisfaction not only in nurturing
and supporting others, but in being nurtured and supported
in efforts which matter to *us*; the right to be fully equipped
-- emotionally, intellectually, materially -- to stand on our
own feet; the power to speak our thoughts and to be really
heard by others; the opportunity to act and to make our
actions effective. Every feminist, whether or not she accepts androgyny as an appropriate symbol, rejects the arbitrary exclusions and limitations which have distorted women's
lives and seeks wholeness for herself and all who are oppressed.

Is it possible to resolve this tension within feminist
thought? I suggest that one step toward doing so is to
recognize that our difficulty arises, at least in part, from
assumptions we have inherited concerning *the basic structure
of actuality* -- assumptions of which we are not yet fully
conscious but which clash with our experience and our visions.
These assumptions, which are metaphysical in the last analysis,
are partly expressed and partly presupposed in traditional
philosophy; they are concretely embedded in our language and
institutions; and they are engraved in our deepest feelings.
They are not explicitly concerned with sexual distinctions;
but the model which they provide is essentially anti-androgynous.

A number of feminists have observed that Western culture
throughout its history has been pervaded by a series of mutually exclusive dualisms, or dichotomies, including (for example) creator and creature, humanity and nature, mind and
body, reason and emotion, activity and passivity, self and
other, subject and object, individuality and relatedness,
life and death. Each of these dichotomies has in some way
been correlated with the dualism of male and female. Furthermore, all these dichotomies have exhibited a pattern of dominance and subordination. One member of each pair has been
seen as more "real," more valuable, or more important than
the other and therefore as inherently or ideally in control
of its "inferior" opposite. The paradigm of dualism and domination and the linking of these various dualisms with the
distinction between male and female have produced the ideologies and social structures which oppress women. It would
seem that neither the proximate goal of feminism -- the liberation of women to full participation in the life
of the human species -- nor its final goal -- provisionally
symbolized as androgynous life -- can be achieved apart from
the abolition of *all* such dualisms. Androgynous life, then,
would be life no longer governed by the paradigm of dichotomy
and domination. But this is a negative definition. Is it
possible to conceive of androgynous life in positive terms?

Let us examine one aspect of the ideal of androgynous
life, to see the difficulties created when we try to concep-
tualize it in terms of the model provided by traditional
thought.

One of the things that androgynous life symbolizes is
the dissolution of a cluster of sexual stereotypes which I
will designate by the terms "individuality" and "relatedness."
In our culture (and in many others), individuality has been
assigned to men and relatedness to women. We are taught that
men are, or should strive to become, *essentially* self-

directing, autonomous, and unique individuals whose needs,
interests, and activities are valuable in themselves. In
contrast, we learn at our mother's knees that women are, or
should strive to become, beings whose existence is *essentially*
constituted by their relationships to others. It is all
right, of course -- indeed necessary -- for a man to have
"relationships" with others, provided that he is not passive
and dependent in these relationships and that they do not
distract him from his primary goal, the pursuit of individuality. And it is all right (in some quarters at least) for
a woman to "have interests outside the home," even to have a
"career" -- provided that even in her "outside" work she puts
relationships to others ahead of all other goals and that she
does not allow such activities to interfere with her essential
task of creating and perfecting her relatedness to husband
and children. The differential assignment of relatedness and
individuality to women and men assumes that no single person
can be both fully an individual and fully related to others.
Yet most of us who have been caught up in the women's movement have experienced moments when we *knew* that to be essentially related to other persons and, at the same time, to be
essentially self-directing, unique individuals whose actions
and concerns are valuable in themselves, are not two conflicting ways of being, but mutually supportive and mutually
necessary aspects of every experience. But when we try to
act on that conviction in our everyday lives -- at work, at
home, even with our friends -- we find ourselves blocked
again and again, not only by the expectations of others, but
by *something in ourselves* which insists that if we wish to be
individuals, we must sacrifice our relatedness to others, and
that to preserve our relatedness we must suppress our individuality. And when we try to explain, even to ourselves,
how all of us might become more androgynous in this sense, we
find it very difficult to say how it is possible.

To understand why this is so, let us look more closely
at the inherited assumptions which underlie our conceptions
of individuality and relatedness.

To be an individual means, in traditional thought, to
exist in a kind of psychic solitude -- at least, a one-way
solitude, like a pane of glass which is transparent from one
side but opaque from the other. An individual is isolated
from the influence of others, while exercising control over
them; he is completely independent, self-sufficient, self-
validating. To paraphrase Descartes' definition of "sub-
stance," an individual is someone who requires nothing but
himself in order to exist. Obviously, no human being can
meet these criteria, but the ideal is there nonetheless,
guiding and shaping our actions, our expectations of others,
and our estimates of ourselves. To the extent that a man
cannot meet such standards, he is apt to feel, and be perceived as, less than "masculine," hence a failure as a human
being.

To be a fully related person, on the other hand, means
in traditional thought to be wholly shaped by and oriented
to others; it means to be entirely and uninterruptedly open
to and supportive of *their* needs, desires, and achievements.
Such a person is defined solely by her relationships; she has
no identity of her own, no enjoyment in her own accomplishments, and no creative effect on the future. To paraphase
Descartes again, a fully related person requires nothing but
others in order to exist. Obviously, no one can consistently
meet these criteria either, but the ideal affects us profoundly. To the extent that a woman is dissatisfied with or
incapable of living up to such standards, she will probably
feel, and be perceived as, "unfeminine" and therefore a
failure.

The metaphysical assumptions underlying this understanding of individuality and relatedness are inherently

anti-androgynous. Not only are the two principles irrecon-
cilable in any single instance of actuality; individuality
(embodied in men) is inherently superior to and dominant over
relatedness (embodied in women). Individuality (man) has intrinsic worth, whereas relatedness (woman) has value only as
support for others. And the content of individuality itself
is determined by these assumptions. Since to be an individual is to be superior and thus dominant, individuality (masculinity) both requires and *consists in* the expression and
enforcement of superiority and domination. That is, "uniqueness" turns out to be comprised of the denigration, manipula-
tion, and destruction of whatever lacks individuality. The
results of a single-minded application of this view are
plain to see in our economic, political and social life and
in the ecological disasters we have created. *This* metaphysics
surely cannot provide a model for androgynous life.

    I now want to turn to Whitehead's concepts of individu-
ality and relatedness, for he challenges those presuppositions of traditional thought which make any ideal of androgyny
based upon them self-contradictory and dangerous.

    I spoke earlier of Whitehead's philosophy as embodying
an androgynous vision. By this I do not mean that the term
"androgyny" appears in his writings, nor even that he was a
feminist in any explicit sense. Indeed, Whitehead appears to
have been oblivious to certain issues of which feminists today are acutely aware, such as the extent of the sexist character of our language, social institutions and practice. Nor
do I wish to claim that a detailed vision of an androgynous
society can be immediately deduced from his metaphysics. Any
such claim would be inconsistent with Whitehead's own view
that the nature of particular forms of existence can never be
deduced from the general principles which characterize all
forms of existence. My aim is more limited: namely, to show
that Whitehead's conception of the fundamental nature of

things provides a general *model* for envisaging androgynous
life.

As stated, the task of metaphysics, in Whitehead's view,
is to describe, as accurately and adequately as possible, the
generic character of those fully actual things which together
constitute the world. And for Whitehead metaphysical analysis reveals that these fully actual entities or facts are not
sticks and stones, nor physical particles, nor even human
beings understood as entities which endure through time. All
these are organized *groups* or aggregates (Whitehead calls
them societies) of these more fundamental actual entities.
According to Whitehead, these primary actual things which
make up the world are "drops" or "buds" (William James' term)
or "pulsations" of experience. Each pulsation is, in this
schema, an individual process, with its own spatio-temporal
boundaries, its own perspective on the past, its own aim and
enjoyment of itself in the present, and its own influence on
the future. And, as such, every actual entity is both a unique and individual occurrence, and an entity which is essentially related to the whole world.

Whitehead's paradigm for conceiving the world as made
up of such pulsations of process is a human occasion of experience . . . such as the experience you are enjoying at
this very moment. An occasion of human experience is not a
static thing, but an activity -- the activity of becoming
what it is. Whitehead speaks of this activity of becoming
as "concrescence", that is, the act of "growing together".
This concrescence is the process by which many diverse experiences (or in Whitehead's terminology feelings) which make
up the past completed world, are integrated into the unity of
a new and unique present occasion of experience, into one,
complete, fully definite feeling. For instance, at this moment, the components of your experience consist of many different feelings, some conscious, some unconscious. There are
the feelings of the sound of my voice, of the specific odor

and temperature of the air in the room, of the surface of the
seats on which you are sitting, of being surrounded by other
people, and so on. And there are other feelings which are
part of your experience now that come from the more remote
past -- such as your feeling about sitting and listening to
someone lecture -- and others which refer to the future. So
your experience at this moment consists of many diverse feelings, and what you are doing is bringing these feelings together in some way to form a unified pattern.

These occasions which you feel in your present process
of becoming are occasions which have already completed their
own acts of becoming. Past, completed occasions were once
themselves activities of self-creation, once subjects synthe-
sizing their own diverse feeling of *their* past world of experience into a unity. Having attained such unity, they now
constitute the past world out of which your present experience arises. They are no longer creative processes of becoming but the completed "objects" there to be appropriated
by you. They are, so to speak, the multiplicity of data
which are given to you for creative synthesis; they are the
elements out of which you are to create your own unique experience. Thus each present moment of concrescence is *essentially related to all past occasions* for they are its primary constituents.

Yet while these past occasions are fixed and given and
hence determining, and you *must* feel them, synthesize them in
some way, *how* you feel them and *how* you integrate them is not
predetermined. Every completed occasion is felt in some way
and with some degree of relevance by you (and by every other
new concrescence) and every new moment of becoming is constituted by its relations, that is its feelings of, the occasions belonging to the past world out of which it arises. Yet
you, in your present moment of experience, feel these past
occasions in your *own* way, from your *own* perspective, for

your *own* purpose, and you thereby synthesize them into a pattern unique to yourself. You, and all other activities of becoming, though constituted by relations to the past, are self-creative and free in those relations. This active, unique creation of the self comes about in accordance with what Whitehead calls your "subjective aim". A subjective aim is an occasion's urge to synthesize its inherited feelings in accordance with some new, novel possibility. In its initial form, your subjective aim is provided by God, who is among the components of your actual world. But even an occasion's initial aim is not fully determinate; that is, it is up to the occasion to decide in which of many different ways it will actualize its general aim. Thus the achievement of an occasion, while made possible jointly by God and antecedent occasion, is, in the final analysis, its own achievement, and this achievement has intrinsic value for the occasion itself. That is why Whitehead calls the final phase of concrescence the occasion's "satisfaction." Thus each concrescent occasion is *essentially an individual* -- self-creative, unique, a being whose "existence is its own justification."[14]

When this act of concrescence has attained its unique, fully determinate synthesis, its life as a subject -- that is, as the active creator of itself -- is over. It perishes. But in perishing as a subject, the occasion passes over to a new kind of existence. It is now an object, a member of the actual worlds of new processes of concrescence. As such, it requires them in turn to take account of it -- to make it part of themselves -- in some way. Thus the value that the completed occasion achieved for itself becomes an element of value in the acts of concrescence which supersede it. In this way every occasion is *essentially related to all future occasions:* to make a difference in the world, for it is part of that world.

Obviously, occasions are not all on the same level with respect to the degree of novelty they can achieve, nor in the extent to which they can transmit their novel achievements to the future. The specific character of an occasion's environment may enhance or severely limit its chances for effective novelty. But despite these differences, all actual occasions exhibit the same three-fold structure: each arises out of and is constituted by its feelings of the past; each is the self-directing subject of its own becoming, attaining its unique satisfaction and enjoying its own self-worth; each contributes its achievements to the future. No occasion exists in "self-sufficient isolation."[15] Yet each is an individual, for there are no "vacuous actualities"[16] no occasions which are merely "vehicles for receiving, for storing in a napkin, and for restoring without loss or gain."[17] Every concrescence is a "moment of sheer individuality, bounded on either side by essential relativity."[18]

Up to now I have been speaking of individuality and relatedness as features of single actual occasions. But a human being is more than a single occasion of experience; more, even, than a linear succession of such occasions. A human being according to Whitehead, is a complex society of concrescent activities, both bodily and mental, so organized as to yield great depth of relatedness and intense individuality. Moreover, the society which is a human being is set within a larger society of societies (its natural environment, including other human beings) which contribute significantly to its individual uniqueness. I must stress that what I have said is a very inadequate account of Whitehead's theory of relatedness and individuality, especially as it applies to human beings. But since a human being is a society of actual occasions, each of which is both fully individual and fully related to the world, it is obvious that the life of every human being, male or female, is both unique and constituted by

its relationships to others. In this limited but important
sense, Whitehead's analysis of the relatedness and individuality of concrescent occasions offers a model for envisaging
androgynous life.

It is clear that Whitehead's model differs radically
from the traditional model which I outlined earlier. Not
only are individuality and relatedness *compatible aspects of
every actuality,* these two principles *require each other.* And
since they require each other, *neither is more "real," important, or valuable than the other.* On the contrary, individuality and relatedness *support and enhance one another.*
The more profound and complex an occasion's relationships to
the world from which it arises, the greater its opportunity
to achieve unique value for itself; and the more unique its
individual satisfaction, the more valuable its potential contribution to the world which supersedes it. What Whitehead
calls the "rhythm of process"[19] at the heart of actuality is a
rhythmic alternation between giving and receiving, between
the appropriation of others for the enrichment of oneself and
the yielding up of oneself for the enrichment of others.
Whitehead's description of the rhythm of process is a metaphysical rendering of what Nietzsche calls "the gift-giving
virtue,"[20] in which the self eagerly pours out the treasures
it has plundered the universe to obtain.

I mentioned earlier a series of dualisms which have pervaded Western culture, all exhibiting a pattern of domination
and subservience and all associated with a dichotomous conception of male and female. I have tried to show that
Whitehead's metaphysics involves a different understanding of
one of these pairs -- an understanding which denies the pattern of dichotomy and domination. In exploring Whitehead's
view of individuality and relatedness, we have also glimpsed
the dissolution of this same pattern with respect to certain
other traditional dualisms: activity and passivity, self and

other, subject and object. If time permitted, it could be
shown that Whitehead dissolves all the destructive dichotomies associated with the distinction between the sexes,
including the dualisms of creator and creature, humanity and
nature, mind and body, reason and emotion -- even the dualism
of life and death.

   This last dualism, the dualism of life and death, is in
my opinion the most important issue awaiting feminist exploration, both because our dichotomous view of the relation between life and death is the wellspring from which all the
other dualisms have arisen,[21] and because this is an issue
about which feminists have not yet begun to think seriously
enough. Although no adequate discussion of the relevance of
Whitehead's metaphysics to overcoming the dualism of life
and death is possible here, certain clues have already been
mentioned. We know that, for Whitehead, the fundamental
actualities which make up the world are living occasions of
experience, brief in duration yet each with intrinsic worth
and self-enjoyment. We know also that each occasion, when it
has completed its process of self-creation, perishes. But in
perishing as a living subject, it does not simply cease to be,
as though it had never lived; the value it has achieved for
itself is appropriated by occasions beyond it, contributing
to their lives something unique and irreplaceable. So the
rhythm of process is the rhythm of living and dying, in which
living occasions are nourished by the dead and occasions
which have perished live on in their successors. No particular occasion is indispensable to the rhythm of process, but
each is a unique individual which *makes a difference,* for
better or for worse. Each is alone in its self-creation; yet
in its aloneness all that has lived is part of itself. Each
is appropriated by others; but in being appropriated it remains its unique self. Just as relatedness and individuality
are not in conflict within us but require and support one

another, so living and dying are mutually enhancing aspects
of every occasion of experience.

It is true that the complex society of occasions which
I call myself will someday cease to exist as *that* society;
this is what we ordinarily mean by "death". Most of us find
it easier to affirm the perishing of our particular occasion
of experience than the death of our enduring selves. Yet th
slightest shift in perspective is all that is needed to enable us to affirm the death of the enduring self also. "Per
spective", Whitehead points out, is another word for "importance".[22] The question is: what importance do we attach
to our enduring selves, in comparison with the vividness of
our lives in the present moment -- that present moment which
as Whitehead says, holds the whole sum of existence, backwards and forwards, within itself?[23] The most basic assumption we have inherited from patriarchal culture, and the one
which feminists may find most difficult to overcome, is that
the enduring self is the true locus of value, and that the
death of that self is our greatest adversary. Until we have
faced this fact honestly and probed the innermost recesses o
our feelings about life and death, we shall not truly have
arrived at the possibility of envisaging androgynous life.

The shift in perspective which would enable us to affir
death will not occur as a direct result of metaphysical inquiry, any more than will the shift involved in affirming th
unity of relatedness and individuality. Feminists are well
aware that when a new idea strikes us as valuable and
right, we are not able immediately to act upon it; that old
habits are not easily discarded; and, most important, that
none of the personal effects of sexism can be overcome on th
purely personal level, since these effects are continually
reproduced in us by our social institutions. The political
is, indeed, personal; and the personal, political.

So androgynous life will not miraculously appear among us just because we find an adequate way of conceptualizing it. For that to happen, we need not only a vision of what we want, but practical plans for creating it. How to bring androgynous life into being is a question I have not addressed not because I think the question is unimportant, but simply because no one can talk about everything at once. Although there are clues in Whitehead's metaphysics which can be helpful in formulating such plans, no metaphysics can give us the concrete methods for effecting social change.

Still, what we think it is possible to achieve by social change is an essential ingredient in bringing it about. If the dichotomies which have been indissolubly linked with sexism in our culture cannot be overcome, then the prospect of overcoming sexism itself seems very dim. On the positive side, while the availability of a model of androgynous life will not create androgyny, it may help us to see more clearly what we are after.

Traditional theology has defined sin as humanity's attempt to transgress the limits of is creatureliness. Feminists might rephrase this in language once used by Charles Hartshorne: "man alone among the animals is able . . . to imagine that he can quarrel with the essential character of the universe while still living in it."[24] The task feminists have set themselves could then be said to be, finally to bring the quarrel to an end. In carrying out this task, Whitehead's metaphysics can be an invaluable ally. Since processes of concrescence are the fundamental actualities of our existence, Whitehead's thought not only provides a way of envisaging an as-yet-unachieved androgynous form of life, it also shows that even now, against the strivings inculcated in us by patriarchal culture, and in spite of the social structures which stand in its way, we are already aware, at some deep level of our existence, that to be is to be androgynous.

If process thought has correctly conceived the basic character of our existence, then what feminists are engaged in
is, in an important sense, the attempt to create something
new; but, in another and equally important sense, we are
trying to make explicit and provide the conditions needed
for a long-delayed flowering of what is already there: the
ever-present androgynous structure of life itself.

NOTES

[1]Alfred North Whitehead, *Adventures of Ideas* (New York:
The Macmillan Company, 1933), 287.

[2]Whitehead, *Process and Reality* (New York: The Macmilla
Company, 1929), 7.

[3]Whitehead, *Adventures of Ideas,* 237.

[4]Whitehead, *Process and Reality,* 243.

[5]Whitehead, *Adventures of Ideas,* 290-291.

[6]Mary Daly, *Beyond God the Father: Toward a Philosophy
of Women's Liberation* (Boston: Beacon Press, 1973), 189.

[7]Whitehead, *Process and Reality,* 24.

[8]Whitehead, *Modes of Thought* (New York: The Free Press,
1968), 6.

[9]*Ibid.,* 3.

[10]Whitehead, *Process and Reality,* 25.

[11]Simone de Beauvoir, *The Second Sex* (New York: Alfred A
Knopf, 1953), 141.

[12]*Ibid.,* 172. (my emphasis)

[13]This perspective was suggested to me by my colleague, Richard Heaton, Professor of Religious Studies at Hobart and William Smith Colleges.

[14]Whitehead, *Modes of Thought,* 109.

[15]*Ibid.,* 140.

[16]Whitehead, *Process and Reality,* 43.

[17]*Ibid.,* 269.

[18]Whitehead, *Adventures of Ideas,* 227.

[19]Whitehead, *Modes of Thought,* 88.

[20]Friedrich Nietzsche, *Thus Spoke Zarathustra* in Walter Kaufmann, tr., *The Portable Nietzsche* (New York: The Viking Press, 1954), 187.

[21]See, for example, Norman O. Brown *Life Against Death: The Psychoanalytical Meaning of History* (New York: Random House, 1959) and Dorothy Dinnerstein, *The Mermaid and the Minotaur: Sexual Arrangements and Human Malaise* (New York: Harper and Row, 1976).

[22]Whitehead, *Modes of Thought,* 9-11.

[23]Whitehead, *The Aims of Education* (New York: New American Library, 1949), 14.

FEMINISM AND PROCESS THOUGHT:

A TWO-WAY RELATIONSHIP

(THE HARVARD UNIVERSITY DUDELIAN LECTURE)

JOHN B. COBB, JR.

In *A Room of One's Own,* Virginia Woolf expounds an idea
she derives from Coleridge -- that all great minds are androgynous. She complains that in her own day major male
writers are so conscious of their virility that they have
nothing to say to women, whereas in Keats, Sterne, Cowper,
Lamb, Coleridge, and above all in Shakespeare, she finds
truly androgynous minds. Her point is not that these people
concerned themselves with the cause of women. Indeed, she
says the "perhaps the androgynous mind is less apt to make
these distinctions than the single-sexed mind."[1] The point
is rather that neither the purely masculine nor the purely
feminine mind can truly create.

Reflecting on recent process thought in this perspective
has forced me to recognize that it has not expressed androgynous thinking. It has been almost exclusively masculine in
style and tone. Here I include most of my own work. And
Woolf is correct that this writing is wanting in the creativity it celebrates. But despite this negative judgment on
my own work, I have come to a renewed appreciation of
Whitehead. Whitehead was, as Mary Daly recognized in *Beyond
God the Father,*[2] an androgynous mind. The power of his

thought lies in his inextricable wedding of intuitive depth and critical intellect. A sentence from such a mind, Woolf rightly says, "explodes and gives birth to all kinds of other ideas,"[3] whereas a sentence written by the purely masculine mind, even if acute and full of learning "falls plump to the ground -- dead."[4]

The writings of an androgynous mind also depict an inclusive world. Recent feminists have stressed the sexual one-sidedness of patriarchal religion and above all its view of God. Alfred North Whitehead did not stress the explicitly sexual character of the Western thought of God, but he attacked its one-sidedness in ways quite parallel to feminist critiques. For him, as for current feminists, the dominant ideas of God in the West, when unmasked, depict a ruthless moralist, an unmoved mover, and an imperial ruler. He sought to replace them with another vision, which he discerned in Jesus, of "the tender elements in the world, which slowly and in quietness operate by love."[5]

One might view Whitehead's move as substituting a feminine for a masculine deity. But Whitehead's completed thought was far more complex and androgynous. He thought in di-polar terms both about the relation of the world and God and about the relation of the two natures of God. In the latter, the primordial nature appears androgynous, whereas the consequent nature appears gynandrous.

In stressing polarities throughout his thought, Whitehead stands in an ancient tradition. In that tradition, Charlotte Clinebell points out, the polarities are almost always so formulated that when one includes masculine and feminine, the list to which one appends the word masculine appears superior.[6] This remains true even though the doctrine, as in the *I Ching* and in Jung, emphasizes the need to transcend dualisms in the unity of opposites. However, when the polarities have been described in Whitehead and subsequently

in a somewhat different way by Charles Hartshorne, this is
not the case. On the contrary, if we add masculine and feminine to these lists, we find the feminine is the actual,
conscious, and inclusive pole in relation to which the masculine is abstract and incomplete.

Whitehead did not add masculine and feminine to his
lists. Indeed, as Mary Daly notes, he rarely uses this kind
of language.[7] The term androgynous is not his. This lack of
sexual language in Whitehead accords with Woolf's comment
that androgynous minds are less apt to make these distinctions than single-sexed minds. Nevertheless, the recent discovery of a speech by Whitehead in 1906 favoring women's suf-
fage pleases me. Although his language would not be acceptable today, and he certainly did not foresee the full depth
of the issues, I believe he did grasp the fundamental principle of liberation. He said:

> I base my adherence to the cause upon the old-
> fashioned formula of Liberty: that is, upon the be-
> lief that in the life of a rational being it is an
> evil when the circumstances affecting him are be-
> yond his control, and are not amenable to his intel-
> ligent direction and comprehension. External con-
> straint upon the rational self-direction of conduct
> is, indeed, inextricably interwoven in the nature
> of things. But wherever it exists, and is removable
> without some corresponding loss of liberty, it is
> the evil, it is the enemy.[8]

Most of us male Whiteheadians have failed to do justice
to the richly androgynous nature of Whitehead's thought. We
have been preoccupied in justifying its use in a male-dominated intellectual climate, and in the process we have distorted it in various ways. We urgently need help from women
to recover what we have obscured.

That women can do that I am sure. The most powerful and
most androgynous Whiteheadian writing I have encountered has
been by Marjorie Suchocki who has shown me depth of meaning
in Whitehead I had missed. Mary Daly's *Beyond God the Fathe*

while preeminently a work of original genius, is also a kind of feminist process philosophy and theology that can open male Whiteheadians' eyes to concrete implications of Whitehead's thought they have neglected.

Thus far I have used the term androgynous as if it were unproblematic. Daly is clearly correct that it presupposes the stereotypes it aims to overcome and retains a masculine bias. The latter problem can be dealt with by reversing the sequence of roots, as in gynandrous, but this does not overcome the dependence on stereotypical meanings. Nevertheless, since the sexual stereotypes exist with continuing powerful effect, we need language that acknowledges our situation and undertakes to move us beyond it. Daly recognizes that these words can contribute to liberation if they are understood as transitional and self-liquidating.[9] It would not be appropriate for a male to use such terms as "gynergy", since they are understood to express a distinctive experience of women. Hence, until helped by Daly and others to a better language, I shall continue to use "gynandry" and "androgyny" to point to the way ahead for women and men.

Daly encourages women to use men's ideas as they are helpful, and she recognizes the attractiveness and congeniality of Whitehead's. She warns that neither they nor those of any other past thinker should be simply adopted as a ready-made theory into which feminist experience could be fitted.[10] I suggest that the model of polarity between feminism and Whitehead may be appropriate to what is needed. Feminism seeks to liberate women from millenia-long oppression in patriarchal society by simultaneously changing consciousness and society. Process thought attempts to understand human experience in its subjective immediacy in full coherence with knowledge about the objective world gained from history and the sciences. Both goals appear laudable, with no apparent conflict between them. Furthermore, process thinkers and feminists direct

their sharpest criticism against similar features of the dominant tradition. Both fight against fragmentation, dualism,
and oppressive force. Both are, in principle, open to change
and fructification. Certainly process thought needs the
stimulation of feminism in order to consider a wide range of
issues to which it has been almost oblivious. And I believe
that as feminists move toward their own solutions of philosophical and theological problems, they can find some features of process conceptuality uniquely helpful.

                                    I

     There is no way to show objectively how feminism is
shaping process thought. Instead I shall tell personally how
I, as one process thinker, have experienced feminism and what
impulses it has given to my developing ideas. The confes-
sional form itself may be more androgynous than my usual
style; perhaps my being pushed to adopt it is already one way
I am indebted to feminism. I am struck by the contrast between my experience and Eugene Bianchi's more conventional
sexist upbringing as he describes it in "Growing up Male: A
Personal Experience."[11] It is well not to forget that even in
Christian patriarchal culture there have been marked diversi-
ties.
     One main surprise of the last few years for me, resulting
from my encounter with feminism, has been to learn the extent
to which the patriarchal system has induced in women feelings
of inferiority and existential incompleteness. I have had to
ask myself why I was so surprised, even incredulous. In
college and especially in the army I heard men belittle women
as mere sex objects, but to my ears it was the men speaking,
not the women, they spoke of, whom such talk cheapened. I had
also vaguely known that women played a smaller role in the
public sphere, but I had no notion that so many had

internalized negative or limited images of themselves; I was truly shocked to realize the innumerable ways our present society continues to dehumanize women. I have had to ask myself why I was so naive.

I believe the deepest reason, apart from sheer insensitivity, is that the image of woman I formed in childhood was based on what I now see as quite a special case: Protestant women missionaries. Retrospectively it is clear that strong women growing up in this country around the turn of the century had few socially acceptable alternatives to marriages in which they had to play subservient roles. Perhaps the most attractive of these options was the Christian mission field. Women organized their own boards of missions, which they ran quite independently of the male-dominated church structures, and they took the liberation of women through the Gospel of Christ as their special task. For this task they recruited unmarried women prepared to devote their lives far from home in strange surroundings speaking a foreign language. One must suppose this did not appeal to the timid! Such women were not the sort who derived their identity from relationships with men. Presumably these women required more courage for their solitary adventures carving new institutions in distant lands than did the men who rarely went without wives. Several such women were part of my childhood. One, in particular, stands out.

Mary Culler White went to China from a small town in Georgia around the turn of the century. I have never known anyone on such close personal terms with God. The result was remarkable personal radiance and charisma. She gave herself each day to God's purposes and then informed God what she would need in order to realize them. God provided what was needed. I myself even as an adult was incapable of denying her anything. One might say she manipulated people, and that, too, would be true. But largely she manipulated by

convincing others that what she asked was indeed needed for
God's work. Since she was quite certain what she was doing
God wanted her to do, she was completely indomitable. I
still find moving her books about her own and other women's
experiences although they breathe a piety never my own.

One incident epitomizes her reputation and character:
Around 1938, when Japanese armies were moving up the Yangtze
River, Mary Culler White gathered her Chinese Bible women
around her and took them to a building in a mountain top
summer resort. The Japanese armies surrounded the mountain
and began to take it. A friend went in consternation to an
American bishop with the news. She had reason to be troubled,
for the Japanese had earned a reputation for raping and
killing defenseless women. She hoped that somehow the bishop
would intercede with Japanese authorities.

The bishop, however, knew Mary Culler White well. So
when told the Japanese would soon reach the summer resort,
he replied: "I'm sorry, there is nothing I can do. The
Japanese soldiers will just have to look out for themselves."
In fact, the bishop's confidence in Mary Culler White was
justified. The soldiers retreated before her wrath with
apologies.

Of course, I knew also missionary wives such as my
mother. And in this case the deviation from the dominant
American type was not so sharply marked. Nevertheless, my
mother shared the missionary vocation with my father. On the
mission field they hired servants for most of the housework
to free both to work outside the home. When the servants had
holidays the whole family shared the work. Even now, with
heightened consciousness, I cannot picture my mother as less
than an equal partner in her marriage.

Even when I returned to Georgia to finish high school
and attend junior college, my positive image of women did not
weaken. I had both men and women teachers, but my best

teachers were women. Not having actually grown up in the
south, Southern racism appeared to me totally unjust and un-
christian. As it did not occur to me to conceal my views, I
found myself occasionally in trouble. But I also found quite
consistently that the people who saw things as I did, who
were prepared to defend their views, were white church women
leaders. My image was of bright, capable, devoted Christian
women working slowly and patiently to bring their duller and
less committed men into a Christian understanding and practice. I still believe these church women are largely to be
credited for having prevented resistance to integration from
being far bloodier than it was.

I was aware that in most families the husband worked and
the wife did not. But since what freedom from working meant
for those with whom I had most contact was freedom to give
leadership to the comunity in socially important matters, I
did not see this as a stigma. From my point of view even today it is outrageous that prestige should go to earning money
when so many of the most important needs of society can be
met only by volunteers. I admire those women who take advan-
tage of their financial freedom to educate themselves about
community and world needs and then do something about them.
Giving that role up to take less interesting, less important
work simply because it pays appears to be capitulating to a
corrupt system. Of course, today I would want to say that it
is just as desirable that the wife earn the money and free
her husband for volunteer work -- *if* he is equally qualified
to do it.

Overall my image of women as shaped through childhood
and youth was more positive than my image of men. In comparison with women, men appeared to me fragile, superficial,
crude, and brittle. The Christian ideals of love, gentleness,
purity, service, compassion for the weak and oppressed, and
active involvement in bringing peace and justice, all seemed

more consistently and adequately expressed by women than men.
Women seemed generally wiser, more whole, more ethical, and
more spiritual. They seemed more competent, more able to ac-
complish their purposes. In academic competition they ex-
celled.

In adulthood I have, of course, seen other sides of
women. I have seen that some are insecure, dependent, demanding, selfish, hostile, materialistic, coarse, vain,
greedy, competitive, moody, vacillating, shortsighted, dull-
witted, spiteful, and so forth. But I have experienced that
simply as a function of individual differences. I have been
often disappointed that so many women fall short of my too
idealistic expectations. As a result I have been too critical of individual women, failing to realize the extent to
which their weaknesses result from social handicaps. I have
not really understood the rage many women experience in the
process of liberation. And I have been particularly slow to
take seriously suggestions that women need special considera-
tions in order to compete fairly with men.

My difficulty with feminism, thus, has not been with its
claim that women can lead us all to a fuller humanity. That
only confirms my earlier experience. My difficulty has been
to assimilate the insistence that, in fact, to date women
have have been largely excluded from full participation in
humanity. I am not arguing that this is not true. Evidence
is overwhelming once it is forced on one's attention. I am
only explaining the great shock it has been to me to face it.
I am only now beginning to appreciate the enormously difficult task a woman faces in becoming truly liberated.

To assimilate these new perceptions theologically has
been almost as difficult as to assimilate them personally. I
had unconsciously prepared myself for this in my somewhat
earlier response to my heightened consciousness about the relation of human beings to nature. There for the first time
I realized that the problem was not only that Christians

failed to practice what they preach or to be appropriately
enlightened in their teaching, but also that some very deep
and generally positive features of the whole Christian movement such as the sacredness of *human* life, were in part responsible for the evil, since they had encouraged us to view
the rest of nature as merely instrumental to human desires.
This realization prompted me to think we need a new Christianity rather than simply renewal or reform. My deepening
intellectual encounter with Buddhism pushed me further in
this direction. Even so, it is my all too recent, shocked
realization that the systematic oppression of women reflects
the explicit teaching and recommended practice of the church
over most of its history that has forced me most thoroughly
to reconsider my role as a theologian. Surely my role was
not to transmit *that* that tradition. One could appeal to
Scripture and especially to Jesus against the worst forms of
sexism, but one must also recognize that the entirety of the
canon is fundamentally patriarchal. Furthermore, Jesus was a
man and the church has committed itself to worship his Father
who is also one with the male Yahweh of the Old Testament. If
this is central to our whole tradition, and if it has on so
many women the effects they now describe, then the new Christianity we need is more radical and fundamental than I had
previously envisaged.

Furthermore, I looked at my own earlier work with new
eyes. Chiefly, I reconsidered the conclusions of my effort
to identify what Christianity most fundamentally is as a mode
of existence.[12] I saw that the self-transcending selfhood of
which I had written had in fact been bound up with the patriarchal cast of thought and experience. I also saw that my
previous emphasis, against Whitehead, on the doctrine of God
as creator, made this element of the patriarchal heritage
part of the essence of Christianity. I did not conclude that
I was descriptively wrong about what Christianity has been at

its best and now is. But I did find my effort to state the
essence of Christianity had boxed me into an account of what
it has been, and that this essentialist thinking had thereby
blocked me from immediately appreciating and accepting the
call the Christian now experiences to enter quite new ground.
So today, particularly as a result of my encounter with feminism, I have begun to attack and oppose all efforts to describe Christianity's essence. The unity of Christianity is
the unity of an historical movement. That unity does not depend on any self-identity of doctrine, vision of reality,
structure of existence, or style of life. It does depend on
demonstrable continuities, the appropriateness of creative
changes, and the self-identification of people in relation to
a particular history. This kind of thinking can be found in
earlier stages of what is now called process theology -- the
socio-historical school of Shailer Matthews and Shirley
Jackson Case; and it is clearly more appropriate to a processive view of all reality. Yet for me it came as something
new. I took seriously my commitments to process thought only
when feminism forced me to recognize that essentialist modes
of thought are untenable.

The feminist recovery of "herstory" has shown historical
progress to be even more ambiguous than I had previously supposed. This heightens the necessity and meaningfulness of a
dialectical reading of history. Each new step of progress is
simultaneously a fall from the previous achievement. As
Sheila Collins says, herstory "shows that the rise of mono-
theism and the development of what has been lauded as the
'ethical impulse' in religious history were not won without
great sacrifice: namely, the rejection of the body as a vehicle for the sacred, the subjugation of women and like
'others' whose experience did not fit the right categories,
and the rape of the earth."[13] Even so, Collins recognizes a
certain inevitability in this historical movement if what we

know as history was to take place. Following Rosemary Ruether, she see "the major role played by the feminine in history to be that of the undifferentiating unconscious, which had to be conquered by the self-conscious, transcending, patriarchal ego in order for civilization to advance in the way that it did."[14]

This parallels the Marxist writing of history which at once regards capitalism as the greatest evil and the highest attainment of history. It fits with the paradoxical Christian idea of the fall upward. But to perceive Christianity as at once the greatest achievement and the greatest calamity of the human race calls on the Christian theologian for uncommon reversals of received habits of mind.

Such dialectical thinking calls for the eschatological justification of the horrors of history. In some ways process theology had always concerned itself with eschatology, but its eschatological ideas have not been seriously historical. Process eschatology has had to do with how all that happens is redeemed within God. Existentialism had celebrated the moment of decision before God, and process theology had appropriated this for itself as well. But liberation theologies in general, and feminism in particular, have warned us that this is far too abstract a way to conceive of salvation. Thousands of years of patriarchal oppression of women are not justified in the existential moment or by the confidence that all is taken up into God. We must envision a fulfilling condition in our actual historical future and live now from that vision. Christianity as a movement must direct itself by its growing and changing vision of what the future can and should be. Yet the major traditions of male-dominated Christianity have lost their visions. All forms of liberation theology address this need, but feminism offers the most convincing and powerful images. When feminism is genuinely integrated with such other concerns as racism, class analysis, and sensitivity to environmental limits, as in Rosemary Ruether's

New Woman/New Earth,[15] it provides the most adequate basis I
now know for a contemporary reconceptualization of the
Basileia, as we may work and pray for it to come on earth.

My encounter with feminism has also exposed the abstract-
ness of process theology in other ways. Process theology is
a philosophical theology striving for conceptual precision
regarding the most fundamental features of reality. It has
sought to ally itself with other forms of theology that have
dealt with concrete issues rather than to generate solutions
to these issues out of its own resources. This is hardly an
adequate procedure at best, but its weakness is glaringly apparent in relation to feminism. Feminist consciousness
raising forces one to see that sexual images are so important
in shaping our minds that to pretend that through philosophical conceptualization we can transcend them is illusory.
Even our purest concepts are refinements of images and their
human meaning is bound up with those images. Sex pervades
the life of imagination.

My confession, then, is that I thought I could work with
concepts and propositions the recognition of whose truth would
generate its own existential consequences. I thought persua-
sion should be addressed to the intellect alone, that any
other appeal was cheating. That is the Socratic-Apollonian
view and a masculine prejudice. The human mind is more than
intellect. In the sense of Coleridge and Woolf theology must
be androgynous. Responsible and convincing shaping of images
certainly should not ignore questions of truth, but as
Whitehead said so clearly: "It is more important that a pro-
position be interesting than that it be true."[16] That requires a style of which process theology on the whole has
been woefully lacking. To realize its potential contribution
process theology badly needs the leadership of women.

II

I come now to the more questionable part of this paper
-- some suggestions to feminists by a male Whiteheadian. I
am proposing a Whiteheadian way of thinking of the relation
of the self or psyche to the body which seems to have constructive relevance to the present stage of feminist discussion.

What is more often called the "mind-body problem" is one
of the oldest and most persistent in the history of thought.
Socrates, through Plato, established for much of Western
philosophy the separateness and primacy of the psyche or soul.
The soul's character and functioning could not be derived
from that of the body, and this indicated that its existence
was only incidentally associated with the body. As in Indian
thought this opened the possibility that the same soul might
be associated with different bodies.

The religious implications were profound. Whereas the
Homeric Greeks had evaluated human beings largely by their
bodily appearance, their physical prowess, and the impres-
siveness to the public of their overt actions, those who followed Socrates believed that the ugly cripple could be a
greater human being than the Olympian athlete or the mili-
tarily successful king. Christianity found this feature of
Socratic thought congenial and took it over. While denying
the possibility of the soul's association with other bodies,
Christianity affirmed the soul's ability to survive death.
Ideas of the immortality of the soul and the resurrection of
the body interacted in confusing ways in the history of
Christian eschatology. Meanwhile, the doctrine of the soul
as something more than the body checked the misogynous tendencies of the male theologians. Women, too, although supposed in some way to be more bodily than men, nevertheless,
were souls capable of being saved by Christ. The same doctrine somewhat checked the theological justification of what

may have been the worst of all forms of slavery, Black
slavery in the United States. Even Black slaves had souls,
and hence, although they could be denied all access to education, they could not be denied hearing the gospel.

Descartes systematized the dualistic tendencies involved
in Greek and medieval reflection on soul and body. What was
not soul or mind was for him a material machine. Since the
only minds were human, animals were, in fact, only machines
with no feelings. Some of his followers are said to have
acted upon his implications with careless cruelty toward dogs.
Much philosophy since Descartes has been shaped by this dualism, either by accepting it or trying to overcome it.

I have indicated the positive consequences of the idea
of the soul as distinct from and superior to the body. Its
existence demands respect, and its worth cannot be measured
by outward appearance. The existence of another soul lays a
claim upon me, and my awareness of being a soul grounds in me
the sense of my own worth and ultimate importance. Jewish,
Stoic, and Christian law express the view that all human beings are souls, and most of the struggles in the West for
justice and freedom from oppression have appealed in one way
or another to this conviction.

The negative side is that the body and the physical
world were denied any similar worth. Alienation from the
body was encouraged. The body and nature were to be conquered
and controlled. Since men viewed women as predominantly
bodily and natural, in spite of the doctrinal check, women,
too, were to be conquered and controlled. It was possible
to tolerate the concrete conditions of degrading poverty and
even slavery on the assumption that what really mattered was
only the salvation of the soul.

In the nineteenth and twentieth centuries, theologians
have come to realize that this depreciation of the concrete human
situation in favor of an immortal soul is not characteristi-
cally Biblical. They began to contrast the Biblical image of

the resurrection of the body with the Platonic doctrine of
the immortality of the soul and to polemicize against the
latter. Some have meant the resurrection of the body quite
literally. Others have been interested only in the way it
symbolizes biblical interest in our bodily condition and thus
undergirds our efforts to feed the hungry and achieve economic justice and political freedom. Those less interested in
retaining traditional images and more concerned to free sexuality from its long repression have recently been contrast-
ing what they take to be the true view: that we *are* our
bodies, with the false one: that we only *have* bodies. With
this insistence they want to direct all our energies towards
realizing the joys of bodily existence and abandoning all
dreams of transcendence or infinity.

I do not doubt this identification of self and body is a
healthy corrective to the alienation of self from body encouraged
by dualistic thinking. But I tremble for its long-term consequences in law and social practice. If we truly *are* our
bodies, then surely we have little ground for egalitarian
thinking. It may be a healing thought for the young, healthy,
and beautiful, but its implications for the old, the sick,
and the ugly differ somewhat.

I do not attribute the negative conclusions I suggest to
either the theological or philosophical advocates of the identity of self and body. But ideas must be taken seriously in
themselves, for if they triumph in the realm of thought it
will not be too long before some jurist or politician begins
to draw conclusions. Hence, I am interested in an alternative
that does justice to the sense in which we transcend our bodies
and have a nature and worth not attributable to bodies as
such, and at the same time avoids alienation from the body
and disdain for the concreteness of embodiment encouraged by
dualism.

As a friendly observer, it has seemed to me that the
same confusion and difficulty is present within the women's

movement, and that here the stakes may be still higher. Women
have suffered even more than men from the dualistic view of
soul and body, and so they have every reason to reject it.
Many see the alienation of self from body characterizing especially males in patriarchal society, and they do not want
to participate in that alienation any more than they have already been forced to do. Indeed, one contribution of women
may be the experience of a wholeness between self and body
that men have lost. This suggests that women might join in
the recent male affirmation of the self *as* the body.

On the other hand, women know much better than men what
it means to be treated chiefly as a body, even to be forced
to think of oneself that way. It is precisely this mode of
experience from which liberation is sought. Women insist
they are persons, subjects, full human beings. And that truth
is not captured in the idea that human beings simply *are* bodies.
Some of the difficulty would be removed if it were understood
that the status of being bodies applied equally and identi-
cally to men and women. Judith Plaskow notes that "if everyone is a body, but no one more than anyone else, then the fundamental category of female otherness, the equation of women
with bodiliness, is undermined and destroyed."[17] Nevertheless,
Plaskow does not end her paper on this note but rather asks
"what, when all is said and done, constitutes a healthy sense
of embodiment?"[18] A sense of embodiment is quite different
from sheer identity, as is clear when the latter is worked
out in the philosophical doctrine of psycho-physical identism.

Other women, reacting against being treated as bodies,
hence, as objects, questing to identify themselves once and
for all as subjects governing their own destiny, take positions which seem to share in patriarchal alienation from the
body. In their eagerness to overcome the image of wife and
mother, dependent as it is on others for definition, they
deny that the biologically distinctive bodily functions of
women are relevant to who they are. Shulamith Firestone sees

the need for "the freeing of women from the tyranny of their
biology by any means available, and the diffusion of the
childbearing role to the society as a whole, to men and other
children as well as women."[19] Here clearly the woman's self
is not the woman's body, and one is left with the impression
that the duality of self and body is a dualism.

Many feminists do not want to abandon the peculiar capacity of women to nurture new life in the womb, and they continue to affirm motherhood. But there is, nevertheless, a
strong tendency to deny that these capacities and functions
are definitive of a woman's existence as subject and person.
Here the alienation from the body may be far less, but a
clearly dualistic tendency remains. The relations between
self and body appear somewhat external to both. The theory
suggested may be that bodily differences between men and
women need not affect human psyches. Viewed as subjects
there need not and should not be, any distinction between
men in general and women in general. What individual differences there are should be allowed to flower.

My point is not that there are deep differences between
two groups of leaders in the movement for women's liberation.
Rather the age-long confusion among human beings about their
relations to their bodies is present in the thinking of feminists too. Many feminists, it seems, see the need both to
attack the dualistic thinking that separates the self from
the body and to affirm that the self is not affected by the
bodily sex differentiation between men and women.

The tension between these two needs is apparent in one
of the most brilliant of the consistently brilliant essays of
Rosemary Ruether, "The Personalization of Sexuality."[20]
Ruether traces the destructive consequences of the separation
of personal existence from sexuality in both asceticism and
libertinism. She sees that the dominant sexual revolution in
its quest to liberate the body from sexual repression is

simply the obverse of this dualism. It represses the consciousness and individual personhood that had been earlier
achieved by repressing the body.[21] Against this she calls for
personalizing sexuality, so sexual relations would express
personal friendship and love. This would seem to require
fully incorporating one's sexual feelings into one's personality. Assuming these sexual feelings are intimately involved with the sexual organs, one would then expect female
and male persons to incorporate different feelings and be
somewhat differentiated as persons. This could lead to some
doctrine of complementarity between the sexes.

Like most feminists, however, Ruether vigorously opposes
any doctrine of complementarity. Of course, procreation requires the complementarity of physical organs but "on the
level of total organisms men and women both equally have all
the organs of thinking, feeling and relating."[22] All distinctions at the level of personality between masculinity and
femininity are "social ideologies."[23] Personal friendship and
love between men and women should not be differentiated from
such friendship and love between members of the same sex, and
since sexual relations should be a function of such friendship and love, there is no difference in value between homosexual and heterosexual acts. Against the conclusion that
differences in sexual feelings would differentiate fully integrated women and men, Ruether presents her position as "a
correction to the false biology presupposed by the doctrine
of complementarity. It is a simple recognition that people
hear with their ears, feel with their bodies and think with
their brains. People don't hear with their vaginas and think
with their penises. Men and women equally have the organs of
psychic activity and receptivity."[24]

Clearly Ruether's basic point is correct, and since the
doctrine of complementarity has always been used by men to
maintain power over women, there is little doubt that her
polemic appropriate. Nevertheless, these formulations cut

in the direction of the dualism which she so ably exposed in
the earlier part of the essay. One portion of the anatomy seems to
be shut off from any contribution to the integrated person.
She neglects the most apparent connecting links, the emotions,
in her analysis. Furthermore, she appears to depreciate the
sex organs in contrast to those of hearing, feeling, and thinking. While the latter contribute to personal existence, the
former do not. This sounds very much like the male experience of detachment of the self from sexuality except that
for Ruether it seems that the sexuality excluded from personal existence will be meekly subservient. Personalization of
sex for Ruether turns out to be complete subordination of
genital sexuality to a personhood from which it is excluded.

The systematic issue is as follows: If we *are* our bodies,
or if our bodies in all their complexity are integral to our
personal existence (mind, soul, self), then the biological
differences between women and men must characterize to some
degree their personal existence. If bodily differences do
not affect personal existence, then there must be a dualism
between body and personal existence; that is, assuming both
exist, they must be external to each other, probably belonging to fundamentally different orders of reality. Feminists
wish, for excellent reasons, to avoid both conclusions, for
the results of both have been disastrous for women. However,
at present, it is not clear just how they avoid both without
inconsistency. And, although in its present dynamic state
the feminist movement can tolerate a great deal of inconsistency, in the long run a clearly defensible position is pre-
ferable.

Furthermore, even if women are not themselves troubled
by this problem, it does perplex men who listen to them. It
is incredible to most men that their sexual feelings could be
so easily transcended. It is equally incredible to them that
the sexual feelings of the two sexes not be quite distinct.
They also find it quite impossible to imagine as irrelevant

the sexual characteristics of either a heterosexual or a
homosexual partner. If feminists want serious attention from
men for their vision of a society in which classification into the two sexes will have no importance for human relations,
they will have to face this incredulity more seriously. We
need a view of soul and body which displays how deeply sexuality,
including the distinctive features of male and female sexuality qualifies the whole psychic life, and yet shows how at
the same time the human self transcends, or can transcend,
this differentiated sexuality.

     In my opinion Whitehead can help develop that kind of
understanding. Whitehead distinguishes animals from plants:
animals emerge from the complex structure of cells as a unified experience with a richness of which no single cell is
capable. In its higher forms this experience is made possible by a central nervous system that feeds stimuli from
many parts of the body to centers in the brain and then medi-
ates what happens in these centers to the muscular system.
The unified momentary experience that receives these stimuli
and decides on appropriate motor responses is "the final per-
cipient" or "the dominant occasion." The animal soul is the
flow of these experiences from birth to death. Apart from
this flow of experience, there is no such "thing" as a soul.
In the case of animals in general, it is probably best to
speak of them as *having* souls. They *are* bodies, which possess souls. The survival and reproduction of the body is the
end; the soul contributes to that end.

     With adult human bings, the role of souls is greatly en-
hanced. Each human experience is greatly influenced by all
the past experiences which make up the individual human soul.
Fresh stimuli in each moment also contribute to human experience, but they are largely selected and interpreted in terms
of categories and interests established in previous experiences. The human soul, like the animal one, serves the body
for its survival and reproduction, but to a considerable

degree it seeks ends peculiar to itself. It enjoys thinking,
for example. It often subordinates the immediate desires of
the body to achieve its own ends as soul. Thus it takes over
the dominant role from the body. The human being *is* a soul
and *has* a body. In this important sense the human person
transcends the body.

But this is a very different transcendence from the dualistic one. The soul is not a thing at all. It is a series
of happenings or experiences. These experiences are not
self-enclosed entities but the coming together in one place
of influences from all over the body along with influences
from earlier experiences. Myriads of bodily events contribute themselves to constitute the new experience that is the
dominant occasion. The relation to the body is not merely
internal to the dominant occasion. It is constitutive of it
in the most radical sense. My experience is not the body but
the unification of bodily experience. Thus what transcends
the body is not something alien to the body but the body's
own achievement of creative unification. Whitehead's philosophy of organism does not identify the person with the body,
but it does affirm that the relation of the person to the
body is thoroughly organic.

On the other hand, the soul which Whitehead also calls
the "living person", is not simply the unification of bodily
experience. It is also alive and self-determinative. It
grasps possibilities relevant to its bodily experience and
through them achieves integrations of which the body is not
otherwise capable. It also introduces novelties that transcend the bodily experience. In this process it can assume
a responsibility for itself and for how it deals with the
body that further emphasizes its transcendence over it.

This means the living human person both organically relates to the body and also transcends it. The extent to
which the organic relatedness is subordinated to transcendent
purposes is one of degree. It is possible for a person to

live largely in and for the body, enjoying a harmony of physical and emotional experience. It is also possible for a
person to subordinate the body and to emphasize and develop
features of personal life that transcend bodily experience.
The introduces tensions into life, but it also facilitates
attaining distinctive human goals in art, culture, science,
and religion.

In one sense, of course, women have always been human
persons. I have used the word person in this sense above.
It means nothing more than the psychic life as a whole, whatever that may be. But this is much weaker than the sense of
person intended by Ruether when she calls for the personalization of sex. The use of person corresponds more to what
Simone de Beauvoir means by Subject. Others speak of ego or
self or essentiality as what patriarchal society has made it
difficult for women to attain. I have elsewhere called the
fullest development of responsible selfhood or Subjecthood
"spirit",[25] and for consistency I shall use that term again
here. In my language, feminists are now rightly insisting
on equal participation in spirit.

I have siad that Whitehead's analysis shows that personal life may be lived either in the most intimate harmony
with bodily experience or in considerable transcendence of
it. When it centers itself most fully on its process of
transcending, the center that develops is spirit. Thus,
spirit may or may not be present in a person's life, but
when it is, it is a transcendent center from which all other
aspects of the personal life are viewed and valued and more
or less integrated.

From this perspective it is a mistake to argue that
apart from socialization sexual feelings are absent in the
psychic life or that the history of the development of these
sexual feelings, together with associated emotions and images,
is identical in females and males. Psychology and biology

are too intimately interrelated, and sex is too important for both, for such dismissal to be plausible. But certainly socialization predominantly determines the form of our sexuality, and either accentuates or minimizes the differences between males and females in our psychic life. Androgyny is no more "natural" than chauvinistic masculinity or submissive femininity, but precisely in recognizing that what is "natural" sets only very flexible limits upon us, we can reshape ideals and control images. We can do so precisely because as spirit we transcend the givenness both of the body and of established modes of thought and because we identify ourselves with this transcendent center. That center transcends the distinction of male and female. In so far as personalizing sex subordinates sexual activity to relations and purposes determined from this center, Ruether is correct that sex differentiation between male and female is relativized.

III

In Section II of this paper I have tried to show how a Whiteheadian conceptualization of self and its relation to the body can help feminists achieve their goal of avoiding both alienation from the body and identification with it. Theoretically overcoming this antithesis, however, does not by itself solve the practical problem; achieving the desirable goal is more difficult than Ruether's essay suggests.

As Ruether recognizes, male depersonalization of sex has characterized all cultures that regard themselves as refined.[26] But in cultures, called archaic, neolithic, or primitive, what she means by personhood, or what I mean by spirit, has not arisen. Hence, up until the present time male sexuality has not been basically personalized.

Ruether suggests that the male's problem is fear of exposing the self to another. On this basis she suggests that by opening themselves to the suppressed feminine aspects of their own natures, men can overcome this fear and consequently abandon their depersonalization of sex. I suspect, on the other hand, that the male's experienced tension between spirit and sex has still deeper roots. Spirit has come into being primarily in the struggle against the dominance of sex (in the broad sense of the Freudian libido) over the psychic life. It sustains itself only in a permanent struggle. And this is not, I think, an accident of socialization. If men adopted Ruether's morality, and restricted sexual activity to their relations with beloved friends, to whom they made long-term commitments, this could only be on the basis of objectifying and controlling sexual appetites. As long as sex is experienced as something to be managed for moral purposes that do not correspond to its spontaneous expression, it will in some measure be experienced as an enemy of morality and hence also of the spirit. It will remain an alien power not integrated into spiritual personality. As long as the male's own sexuality is objectified as alien to his spiritual personality, there will be a tendency to view the sexual partner as something distinct from the spiritual partner. The "resurrection of the body", through the despiritualization of the psychic life has profound appeal to the male because it so often appears to be the only road to psychosexual harmony.

Herbert Richardson presents what, from the male point of view, is a more promising approach to the personalization of sex. He points to a developing custom of adolescent petting in which sexual relations are not allowed to develop apart from or beyond personal relations.[27] That means the male expresses his sexuality only as a part of his integrated personality. In this case he incorporates his male sexuality fully into his personality.

Richardson's suggestions point to the overcoming of the male experience of dualism of sex and personhood in a way that Ruether's do not. They would overcome man's need to objectify his own sexuality together with its concomitant degradation of women. But it would leave us with the complementarity of male and female persons, which feminists generally reject. My suggestion, however, is that we should accept the need for men to achieve this kind of integration. We can then recognize that the true self, I, or spirit transcends complementarity as well. What *I* am, finally, need not be a function of my being a male. And I can relate to you at the level at which your femaleness or maleness is no longer relevant. This vision is not uncommon where the experience of spirit is vivid. In the eschatological community there is neither male nor female.

Just as women are demanding an equal place of leadership in the public order while refusing to accept the basic structures by which that order has been constructed, so also women are demanding full participation in spiritual personhood while refusing to accept the enormous price in inner tension and outward oppression that men have paid for it. What does this mean? Sometimes I view it cynically as the childish desire to have one's cake and eat it too, as the unwillingness to recognize that every mode of existence and social order is ambiguous to its core, as the refusal to admit that every gain is accompanied by loss. At other times I view it as the last great hope of humankind. The cynical view is all too easy to argue. I shall not bother to do so. To have any hope of responding to our present global crisis we must nourish a hopeful vision. Of those now proposed, feminism offers the most compelling. I will close with my own appropriation of that vision.

The relatively harmonious, relatively egalitarian cultures of our primitive ancestors lived predominantly under the maternal principle. The Great Mother Goddess was both

origin anf destiny. Such a society was relatively static and
limited in terms of the variety of human potentials it could
realize. It was the male who experienced these limitations
as restrictions and struggled free from them. This required
transcending his own bodily functions, especially his sexuality. It required division of labor and complex structures
of government. In fact, and perhaps of necessity, it involved
the subordination of women and widespread slavery as well as
hierarchical structures throughout society. Although the
Great Mother Goddess continued to play a large role, the
fullest development of patriarchy required worship of the
Creator Father. This patriarchy has enormous cultural
achievement to its credit as well as unimaginable horrors.

Now for some time we have been living in the decay of
patriarchal society. Men have been forced to recognize that
the finest accomplishments of this society are destined to
destroy the human race. The tensions between the power
structures through which they have enforced their will, on
the one side, and the moral principles which, through their
transcendence, they have adopted, on the other, have destroyed the convincing force of both. Men no longer believe
either in their power or in their ideals. They have largely
lost the sense that they can control their own destiny. They
no longer care for their transcendence. Lacking transcendent
purposes they live for immediate pleasure, comfort, and status. All of this is expressed in the decay of patriarchal
religion.

The feminist movement incisively criticizes all dimensions of patriarchy. It points back with pride to that ancient time when the maternal principle dominated culture. But
it recognizes as a temptation any thought of return to that.
It is as full persons and not as mothers that women now claim
their equal place. That entails a positive appraisal of the
patriarchal achievement at its most fundamental level. But
it does not mean accepting either oppression or decadence.

It means refusing either to go back to a possibly idyllic past in which the psychic and social life were more harmonious or to accept the dualism of spirit and body with all of its destructive results. The adventure of transcendence will turn toward transforming the fruits of patriarchal history so that repression of nature and the body, once necessary to their attainment, will no longer be required. Nature and the body are to be liberated not through sacrificing transcending spirit but by fulfilling it. The wholeness sought is an inclusive consummation of the whole, terrible course of history through which alone history can be given positive meaning.

It may have been necessary that the great adventure of civilized history has thus far been under patriarchal auspices. There may now be reason that the new adventure toward inclusive harmony should be led by women. Certainly what is required is an upsurge of archetypal feminine aspects, and certainly the image of inclusive harmony toward which we should move is feminine or gynandrous. It may be that the recent emergence of feminism has not only world-historical but also eschatological meaning.

NOTES

[1]Alice S. Rossi, ed. *The Feminist Papers* (New York: Bantam Books, 1974), 649.

[2]Mary Daly, *Beyond God the Father* (Boston: Beacon Press, 1973), 188.

[3]Rossi, 650.

[4]*Ibid.*

[5]Alfred N. Whitehead, *Process and Reality* (New York: Macmillan Press, 1929), 520.

[6]Charlotte Clinebell, *Some Existential Perspectives on the Alienation of the Sexes: Toward a Gynandrous/an Androgynous Society* (unpublished Ph.D. dissertation, Claremont Graduate School, 1976), 197-200.

[7]Daly, 21.

[8]Alfred N. Whitehead, a speech given to the Cambridge Women's Suffrage Association, 1906. "Liberty and the Enfranchisement of Women," *Process Studies,* VII/1. Spring 1977, 37.

[9]Mary Daly, "The Courage to Leave," *John Cobb's Theology in Process,* ed. by David Ray Griffin and Thomas J.J. Altizer (Philadelphia: Westminister Press, 1977), 89. See also Mary Daly, "The Qualitative Leap beyond Patriarchal Religion," *Quest* 1:4 (Spring 1975) 29-32.

[10]Daly, *Beyond God the Father,* 37, 188f.

[11]Eugene Bianchi and Rosemary Ruether, *From Machismo to Mutuality: Essays on Sexism in Woman-Man Liberation* (New York: Paulist Press, 1976), Chapter II.

[12]John B. Cobb, Jr., *The Structure of Christian Existence* (Philadelphia: Westminister Press, 1967).

[13]Sheila Collins, *A Different Heaven and Earth* (Valley Forge: Judson Press, 1974), 141.

[14]*Ibid.,* 115.

[15]Rosemary Ruether, *New Woman/New Earth* (New York: Seabury Press, 1975).

[16]Whitehead, *Process and Reality,* 395-396.

[17]Judith Plaskow, "Our Bodies/Our Selves: Meditations on a Theme," (an unpublished paper read at the American Academy of Religion meeting, 1976), 17.

[18]*Ibid.,* 18.

[19]Shulamith Firestone, *The Dialectic of Sex* (New York: Bantam Books, 1970), 238.

[20]Bianchi and Ruether, *From Machismo to Mutuality.*

[21]*Ibid.,* 77.

[22]*Ibid.,* 83.

[23]*Ibid.,*

[24]*Ibid.,* 84.

[25]Cobb, *The Structure of Christian Existence.*

[26]Bianchi and Ruether, *From Machismo to Mutuality,* 70.

[27]Herbert W. Richardson, *Nun, Witch, Playmate: The Americanization of Sex* (New York: Harper & Row, 1971).

OPENNESS AND MUTUALITY IN

PROCESS THOUGHT AND FEMINIST ACTION

MARJORIE SUCHOCKI

Early in graduate school I found myself in a perplexing situation. My only association with Whitehead had been an abortive reading of *Process and Reality*.[1] After the first one hundred pages, it occurred to me that I was not at all sure what I had read, whereupon I went on to more comprehensible texts. Imagine my mystification, then, when my offered comments in classes would be greeted with, "oh, you're into process," or "obviously you have a Whiteheadian perspective." In due time I took a course on Whitehead, and this time, under John Cobb's tutelage, *Process and Reality* came alive: Whitehead was describing *my* experience of the world. Suddenly I had found a philosopher who knew the same world I did, but who had the power to penetrate the dynamics of that world, and to formulate its nature in terms of a comprehensive metaphysics. Since then, I have consciously incorporated into my life structure what was implicit in my views for so long. I do indeed interpret the world from a "Whiteheadian perspective."

I introduce this paper so personally because I think it profoundly important to emphasize the existential quality of Whitehead's thought. I come to it not as an interesting speculative system, though it is surely that, but from my need to understand my world in holistic terms through a conceptuality which fits my experience. Whitehead gives me that conceptuality, describing existence as a creative response to the past and towards the future, with that response being thoroughly and integrally relational. In this conceptuality, relationships are illumined as being weighted toward a mutual enhancement. Through relationships, one continuously adds to the completion of others through the completion of oneself.

In such an understanding, the whole of reality may be characterized in terms of mutuality and openness. Mutuality indicates the interrelationships of existence whereby value is created through interdependence. Openness indicates the orientation of existence to ever-new forms of value; the future is the creation of new values through the creative response to relationships of the past. Throughout, this universe of mutuality and openness is pervaded by the creatively interacting presence of God.

Just as this process perspective meets my existence, I have increasingly found myself working from the implications of another perspective as well -- not in a way which vies with my process vision, but in a blended harmony since the two perspectives unite in my own experience. The second perspective is feminism. I first came upon process philosophy while I lived in the relatively restricted spheres of home and school; for me at that time the world of metaphysics felt closer than the seemingly distant world of social structures. The "distance" was indeed deceptive. As my awareness of the pervasive presence and importance of social structures has grown, so has my awareness that in many ways the social structures within which I live violate my sense of rightness. Feminists address precisely these points of violation by calling for new structures which will emphasize the worth of persons rather than roles, of interdependence rather than dominance, and of creative openness to the new rather than unquestioning

social system
and
metaphysical vision

64   *FEMINISM AND PROCESS THOUGHT*

repetition of the past. The address to humanity on this
level, insofar as it succeeds, will result in a social structure in keeping with the ethical implications of a process
metaphysics. The two perspectives, process and feminism,
meet in the emphasis of values related to mutuality and openness.

Since I thus find process and feminist modes of thought
to complement each other in my own experience, I would like
to develop two specific possibilities through which each mode
might enrich the other. The first concerns the problem of God:
the intense male orientation of traditional doctrines of God
reinforces quite effectively the subordination of women.
Since "God," "maleness," and "subordination of women" have
been so inextricably interwoven, one might think all doctrines
of God anathema to feminists. On the other hand, if feminists
simply relinquish doctrines of God as unredeemable, then the
negative effects of existing doctrines simply continue. The
process development of a notion of God is not only compatible
with feminist values, but it provides a metaphysical grounding
for them. Hence process counters the sexism of traditional
doctrines, and can be enriching to feminists.

The complementing mode whereby feminists are necessary
to process philosophy lies in the arena of social action. The
philosophy espouses ideals of openness and mutuality; feminists commit their lives to the enactment of these values in
society. No philosophy dare separate itself from the ethical
implications of its system; through feminist action, the
ideals of process thought enter into reality. I am not im-
plying that the philosophers of process can let feminists do
the work of actualizing these values in their stead. Far to
the contrary: openness and mutuality are truly valued to the
extent that they galvanize action toward achieving these
ideals. Women have been socially excluded from the full implications of these values. Only as women and other excluded

groups can participate fully and equally in society are openness and mutuality more than empty rhetoric; therefore, those
who are committed to process modes of thought need alignment
with the ethical action of feminists.

I

The process concept of God provides a metaphysical
grounding to the values of openness and mutuality so essential to the feminist program. In addition to this, the concept can be further developed to answer the problem of the
relationship of God to sexuality and to human characteristics
traditionally related to sexuality. In both regards the process concept is not only non-sexist, but anti-sexist.

The process model of God is developed through three key
notions: God as primordial, God as consequent, and God as the
unity of the primordial and consequent. All three are integrally related to Whitehead's analysis of existence as process: existence occurs in "drops of experience," with each
"drop" coming into existence through its relational feelings
of the past. These feelings unite into a new possibility for
existence, becoming actual through the unification, which is
in fact the reality. One can therefore discuss a single at
atom-like bit of existence as being 1) feelings of the past,
2) integration of those feelings through a grasp of what is
possible given those feelings, into 3) the new unified reality. For systematic reasons, Whitehead's model for God must
reverse the procedure. In the model, God "begins" with 1) a
unified feeling of all possibilities whatsoever, called the
primordial nature. This aspect of God in the model is as
eternal as possibilities. Since the possibilities are unified in God's valuation, there is a primordial completion of
beauty and harmony in God. The analog to the feelings of the —
past for God would be 2) God's feelings of the world, called

the consequent nature. Whereas the primordial nature unites God's feelings of all things possible, the consequent nature is simply God's feelings of all things actual. There must then also be 3) God's integration of the actual with the possible, or the unification of the primordial and consequent natures into the single reality which is God.

How does such a model ground the feminist valuation of openness and mutuality? Consider first the feminist value of openness. In a feminist context, openness means recognizing new possibilities of identity, new possibilities of actualizing one's potential, new possibilities of relating to others in terms of personhood rather than stereotypes or roles. It connotes a positive valuation of novelty relative to enriching and expanding the boundaries of human experience. There is a future orientation to such openness, for it requires a vision of what might be in contrast to realization of what is.

Now consider the value in relation to the primordial nature of God. In Whitehead's model, the primordial nature is God's vision of all possibilities as sheer possibles. This, of course, requires a complexity beyond degree, for the only limitation upon possibility is actuality. That is, a given actualization is what it is, and therefore has cut off the possibility of its being anything else -- to choose to become one thing by the very nature of the deed excludes becoming another. Actuality is the limiting factor. In a realm of pure possibility, such as the primordial nature, there are no limits. To visualize a realm of completely abstract possibilities is to visualize the entire range of possible relationships. There is therefore an infinite openness to the vision.

This infinite openness to the possible, however, is posited as taking place within the primordial vision of God. That is, the actuality of God is the locus of the vision. If actuality limits possibility, is it not the case that the fact that possibilities are visualized through and in the actuality of God

is indeed a limitation?   The limitation resulting from the
actuality of God is not the exclusion of possibilities, but
the ordering of possibilities.   That is, the possibilities
are valued in terms of possible richness.   Each possibility
receives its divine valuation according to its possible enrichment of all other possibilities; each is valued, therefore, in terms of goodness.   Given the infinite range of possibilities in the inclusiveness of the vision, it is not that
goodness can be restricted to a small sphere of possibles;
goodness depends upon enrichment with regard to the whole
realm of possibility.   This valuation in terms of goodness
is precisely the unifying factor of the vision; without it,
chaos would mark the multiplicity of possibles.   As it is, if
all possibles are felt by the one reality of God in terms of
goodness, this very valuation is the ordering of possibilities
into the singleness of a world of possibility within the divine vision.   The openness of God to possibility is therefore
infinitely ordered according to goodness.

Openness is not confined to the primordial nature of God,
but relates as well to the consequent nature. Here Whitehead's
model portrays God's receptive feelings of the world. In God,
these feelings are necessarily wholly inclusive, so that
every element in the world is felt in its entirety by God.
There is nothing too minute or insignificant for the divine
care; whatsoever comes to pass in the world is felt by God
through the feelings of the consequent of nature.   God feels
the world.   Just as the primordial nature demonstrates God's
supreme openness to possibility, the consequent nature demonstrates a supreme openness to actuality.

If both primordial and consequent aspects of God can be
understood as paradigmatic instances of openness, even more,
must God, in integrated unity, also be understood through
this value.   The world, felt by God, meets its destiny in God.
My reference here is to those concluding pages in *Process and*

Reality where Whitehead speaks of the world being woven by
God into the primordial harmony.[2] This integration of the
world within the primordial vision fulfills two functions
within the philosophy: first, it accounts for the ultimate
unity of God, such that God can be spoken of in terms of
actuality, and second, it accounts for the way possibilities
within the primordial nature are felt by God in terms of relevance to the actual world. This feeling of relevance in-
auguarates the mediation of possibilities to the world, or
the effect of God upon the world.

Openness is integral to this unification of the world
within God's primordial vision. God feels the world as it
is, from every standpoint, without qualification. This means
that God feels the joy and the pain, the justice and the injustice, the good and the evil of the world from every perspective the world affords. God's feelings of actuality,
however, is in terms of possibility: God feels "what is" in
terms of "what might be." This is necessarily the case, if
God's feelings of the actual are integrated with feelings of
the possible. If feelings of the possible are in terms of
goodness, then the integration of the actual with the possible will relate the "isness" of the actual world with its
own best "might be" from the possible world. This "might be,"
so intimately associated with God's evaluation of the world,
draws upon the infinite openness of God to both possibility
and actuality; it is the best that is possible for the particular world at a given point in its history. In the dynamics of process, God must affect the world as well as the
world affecting God. If the world affects God through its
actuality, God affects the world through the provision of
possibility. God's feeling of the "might be" for every con-
ceivable standpoint in the world follows from the divine unification of the consequent and primordial natures, and issues
into divine guidance of the world into new possibilities of
richness and goodness.

wh opnem = feminist openness?

If this openness of God is associated with the openness so valued by feminists, it might be suggested that the compatibility between the two is natural rather than forced. God, in the process vision, is the ground of openness, and the source of new possibilities for the world. Lest it be objected that there is an undue dependence upon God for one's possibilities in such a vision, it must also be pointed out that there is a dependence of God upon the world. Possibilities for the world must be shaped according to the actuality of the world. Possibilities irrelevant to the world are *nukes* powerless, even in the vision of God, with respect to the world. Only as persons begin to act upon the ideals of openness, turning what is possible into actuality, can God integrate that new actuality into a vision which will elicit still further relevant modes of openness for the world.

The value of mutuality is also grounded through the process model of God. Within the feminist context, mutuality is the sensitivity between persons that is to characterize human relationships. Mutuality indicates structures of society whereby governance does not consist in hierarchical domination carried out for the preservation of an elite, but is rather a democratic care for the good of all.

I have already noted that the primordial ordering of all possibilities in the primordial nature of God is in terms of goodness. This goodness is an ultimate unity, a togetherness of all possibilities according to God's valuation. Each possibility is understood in its relation to every other. None is valued for its own sake alone; rather, its valuation is precisely its possible role in relation to every other possibility. This constitutes the unity of the primordial vision, the ground of the togetherness of the otherwise chaotic realm of sheer potentiality. Mutuality -- that togetherness through which each participates in the other to the enrichment of all -- has its germinal reality in the divine envisagement of all

possibilities. The openness of God to all possibility therefore finds its unity through the sense in which God feels
each possibility in terms of relationships to the others. No
greater form of mutuality could be conceived for such a realm.
It is absolutely essential for the unity of God.

Mutuality also relates to the consequent nature of God.
Again, in Part V of *Process and Reality* Whitehead suggests
that God receives the world in a "unison of immediacy" which
is the "retention of mutual immediacy."[3] "Immediacy" is
Whitehead's peculiar term for the subjectivity of experience;
it is the subjectively felt identity of every drop of experience. God has "immediacy," and every particle of existence
likewise has "immediacy." If God receives the world in a
"unison of immediacy," does this not mean that the subjectivity of the finite occasion is taken into the subjectivity of
God? And if there is a "retention of mutual immediacy,"
could this not indicate that both immediacies are retained in
mutuality? That is, the finite is not sacrificed to the infinite; rather, the finite and the infinite exist in complementarity. Is this not an ultimate mutuality between God and
the world within the divine nature?

One must push this mutuality even further in light of
the fact that God feels not selected actualities, but all
actualities. Since they are all felt by the subjectivity
which is God, would it not be the case that insofar as every
finite reality feels its own immediacy in and through God, it
would feel all the other immediacies in God as well? The mutuality would then not be simply between one actuality and
the divine subjectivity, but between every actuality within
the divine subjectivity. How could mutuality be greater?

Actuality, however, is integrated with possibility in
the unifying activity of the divine nature. What is, is integrated with what might be. The goodness of the primordial
nature is not at all restricted to that aspect of God, but
permeates the entire reality of God. The felt world, rooted

now in the subjectivity of God, moves into the valuation of the primordial vision. Judgment and justice, goodness and beauty mark the transformation of the world from the "is" to the "might be." If all possibilities are valued by God in relation to the whole, and if each actuality in the world feels through the medium of God its relationship to all other actualities, then the unification which everlastingly occurs in God is the blending of both forms of mutuality into one. The catalytic force of this union of mutualities is the dynamism of the universe whereby new possibilities continuously move into relevance for the world. Mutuality in its ultimate sense pushes toward new and deeper forms of mutuality. The integration of the world within God's primordial vision in the fullness of mutuality is the source of the world's vision of new forms of mutuality and richness within human society.[4]

Given such a grounding to the value of mutuality in the nature of God, it can hardly be argued that the doctrine of God is necessarily anti-feminist. Rather, to hold to an understanding of God which actualizes the value of mutuality to a supreme degree can inspire our own efforts to achieve new degrees of mutuality within our existence. The visions which we have of mutuality are not insubstantial fluffs of the imagination, rooted only in the whims of political history. Instead, feminist insight and action are rooted in the flow of reality toward deeper forms of value, grounded in the way of God with the world.

If the process conceptuality answers feminist concerns regarding the relationship of God to feminist values, it also addresses areas which are of equal concern to feminists. These are first the relationship of God to sexuality and second the divinizing of sex-stereotyped characteristics. Both problems arise from the traditional association of God with maleness. If God is fundamentally understood in terms of masculinity, and if masculinity is defined in terms

which are restricted either biologically or sociologically to
men, then men are perforce godlike. Male stereotypical characteristics are divinized by association with God. When God
is further understood in terms which might characterize a
beneficent tyrant ruling with unquestioned and unquestionable
authority, there is an easy transition toward social structures in which men, godlike, rule over others. The ultimate
"others" in the human scheme are obviously women, since they
alone are decidedly not men. What is the relationship of God
to maleness and toward sexuality as a whole within the process conceptuality?

With regard to sexuality, consider again that the supreme unity of God follows from the sensitivity with which
God feels the many forms of possibility and actuality in
terms of mutual enrichment. In God, the many are unified
into one. God's feeling for possibility in relation to actuality issues into the everlasting creativity whereby a world
is brought into being which has the possibility of reflecting
the divine nature of openness and mutuality in harmony. If
the divine harmony is a togetherness of diverse realities,
with each reality retaining its distinctness yet finding its
full valuation in relatedness to all others, what does this
say about the kind of world which could best reflect the divine harmony? Is not sexuality a key way by which the diversity of two are brought together in a new unity which offers depths of richness and mutuality? Perhaps it is the
case that human sexuality, whereby two move toward actualized
union, is a finite reflection of the harmony of God. The
creation of humanity in terms of distinctions which find
within themselves an urge toward mutuality and unity might
be considered as an inner large lure from separateness to togetherness, akin to the complex togetherness which is God.
When relations between persons consciously reflect a unity
based upon mutuality of respect and sensitivity, then this

union might indeed be the achievement of the image of God in *Trad.*
human relationality.

The image, however, depends upon the relational mutuality. The focus is not upon sexuality per se, but upon the
achievement of harmony which sexuality uniquely allows. From
the unified harmony of God, who is one, comes the possibilities of harmony for the world, which are many. Within this
conceptuality, God relates to the distinctions of sexuality
through the creative impulse which moves from the complex
unity of God to the diversity of creatures who themselves
respond to the impulse to create a new form of complex unity
in their own interrelatedness.

There is no sense in which the above could be reduced to
sexism, for there is no provision for vaunting one sex above
the other. On the contrary, this view is anti-sexist in its
very focus upon mutuality. Neither man alone nor woman alone
represents God; that high function occurs only in the process
of two relating to each other in harmony as one.

To relate sexuality to God by considering the divine
unity as the source of sexuality is to emphasize the role of
the primordial nature of God in creation. To consider the
consequent nature highlights the sense in which God is related not to sexuality, but to masculinity and femininity
with regard to qualities. Insofar as God receives the world
through the feelings of the consequent nature, God receives
the reality of our experiences as men and women. One could
push this further and state that insofar as God receives the
world in that "retention of mutual immediacy," God ultimately
receives ourselves. Our destiny is God. If, however, God
receives women and men into the divine nature, then it is
also the case that God feels the qualities which women and
men have actualized. Let me put the matter concretely: I am
a woman; I am therefore feminine. Whatever I think and do is
feminine simply on the basis that I am, indeed, a woman. God

receives me into the divine nature. There is therefore femininity in God insofar as I and every woman contribute our
own concretely feminized qualities to God in mutual immediacy.
The same could be said for every man with regard to masculinity.

Such a view presupposes that there are many possibilities within the premordial nature which relate to being human.
Other than "male" and "female," the possibilities are neu-
tral as to gender, requiring only the existence of male and
female for human relevance. Caring, thinking, planning,
hoping, nurturing, creating, organizing -- such are the possibilities given to humanity. For a man to choose to care is
then to masculinize the caring, or actualizing a supposed
"feminine" nature within him, the man is simply giving masculinity to his own particular caring. The quality does not
feminize the man; rather, the man masculinizes the quality
for his own particular existence. Likewise, for a woman to
care is to give feminine reality to the quality, making caring
a facet of her own unique personality, thus feminizing it. In
neither case does either the man or the woman legitimately
universalize the particular: each instance of caring is tied
to time and place, and cannot be generalized to all people in
all times and places. Until the quality moves from possibility to actuality, it is neither masculine nor feminine; when
the quality moves into actuality through human choice, it is
then either masculine or feminine according to who has made
the choice. Therefore, whatever any woman does is feminine,
and whatever any man does is masculine. The abstract possibilities take on femininity or masculinity only in the complexity of actuality.

If such is the case, then qualities are only deriva-
tively masculine or feminine, not inherently so. Insofar as
God receives women and men into the divine nature, God also
receives whatever qualities they have masculinized or feminized in their existences. There is therefore a derivative

presence of "masculinity" and "femininity" in God through the consequent nature. This derivative presence gives a real basis for utilizing masculine and feminine imagery with reference to God, but it does not provide a basis for assigning priority to one form of imagery over the other.

While we may speak of God's reception of human qualities through women and men, this in no way limits the qualities of God. For instance, if women feminize the quality of caring through actualizing this attribute, and men likewise masculinize the quality, it would be the case that God, in caring, divinizes the quality. If we consider God's qualities in this light, then "divinity" functions analogously to "masculinity" and "femininity", and "divine" functions analogously to "male" and "female". Care must be taken, then, as we use masculine and feminine imagery with regard to God that we do not reduce God either to humanity or to the human range of qualities. God as primordial and consequent is the source and end of humanity; God is the creative ground calling humanity with all its distinctions into being, and the creative destiny to which humanity returns.

II

It is to be hoped that this discussion of a process concept of God can answer feminist concerns with regard to feminist values and feminist sensitivities concerning the relation of God to masculinity and femininity. If, however, process thought can be of value to feminism in its doctrine of God, feminists also offer a rich and irreplaceable contribution to process. This contribution rests in the area of concrete social action. While it is happily true that process philosophy is receiving a wider and wider application in such concrete areas of experience as education and psychological

counselling, I am not aware of many ways the ethical implications of process thought are finding concrete realization in
the arena of social justice. In this wide sphere, process
thought might appear as just one more abstract ivory tower
having little relation to the power structures of daily life.
The validity of any system of thought, however, rests not
only with its coherence and consistency, but most importantly
with its applicability to daily concerns. The system must
illumine those concerns in a directive way, adding to the enrichment of life. Only as the system is related to the realities of action in the broad spheres of experience is that
system validated.

Feminists call and act for social change; these changes
are in fact consonant with the ethical implications of process philosophy. The openness and mutuality which I have
described as grounded in the process doctrine of God must
also be reflected in society. The fact that most feminists
make no conscious association between their work and such a
concept of God does not negate the existing affinity. Feminists who call for openness and mutuality in the structures
of society are working toward concretely realizing values
which not only permeate the process metaphysics, but find
their deepest foundation in the process notion of God.

The value of openness in process terms is simply that:
openness. The ways of openness are relative to the conditions which pertain to society and individuals within society
in definite times and places. The contribution of feminists
to process thought is in the new definition of what openness
means here and now. Through feminists -- and indeed, all liberation groups -- openness is defined, actualized, and con-
cretized. This concretization of openness then must lead
to new forms, for openness always pushes beyond any one form
of actualization. Feminists define and actualize the moving
edge of openness.

As femininsts translate openness to the realm of social
ethics, they call for releasing opportunities from the confines of arbitrary strictures. Openness is the reality of
alternatives made available to persons; it is the enlargement
of real potentiality in the actual world. There are, of
course, many factors which narrow the range of real possibilities. Insofar as these factors are legitimate, they indicate directions of choice which fulfill the individual's capacities and needs in keeping with the needs of society as a
whole. Insofar as these factors are illegitimate, as sexism
is, they function toward restricting opportunities for some
members of society, not for the enrichment of the whole but
to sustain an elite. Feminists address themselves to this
restriction of the real potentiality of women. Through con-
sciousness-raising on the individual level, and political
action on the societal level, feminists work to increase
available opportunities for women. Of course, men as well as
women stand to benefit from this widening of opportunities.
Real potentiality increases for both women and men as society
achieves new openness of opportunity.

Insofar as openness of opportunity is achieved, another
form of openness emerges as well. When roles are defined
traditionally, much concerning any role is simply assumed.
Creativity can easily be stifled when long established custom
defines a particular role. For instance, the office of minister or priest has long been understood primarily as one filled
by a man. When a women finds this office to be an open possibility for her, and actualizes that possibility, she not only
achieves a new openness in her own life, but she re-opens the
role of minister or priest in a whole series of dimensions.
By shattering the traditional confines of the role, she opens
it to new dimensions of meaning. This takes effect not only
with reference to the office itself, but also with reference
to the many institutional functions surrounding the office --
not the least of which are the seminaries which train persons

for it.   Thus openness engenders further modes of openness;
as feminists achieve new openness of opportunities, we stand
at the brink of creativity whereby we might realize new depths
of richness in hitherto relatively static roles.

There is yet another dimension to the openness of opportunity being achieved by feminists. This concerns the
role identity of children growing up within society. Social
expectations of each generation are shaped by the roles and
functions of the adults in the society. Reams of rhetoric
concerning freedom of opportunity are of little value if in
fact the role models presented to children confirm restrictions of opportunity. As women actually enact their liberation, they provide the reality of freedom which can then
shape the consciousness of the next generation. There should
be a cumulative effect to the work of feminists in creating a
society where persons are increasingly open to new opportunities.

What is the value of mutuality as it is translated into
ethical action? I see at least three major ways feminists
call for a concrete actualization of this value in the fabric
of society.

First, women are calling for a bonding together to
achieve new goals. Insofar as women heighten their sensitivities to one another's concerns, a mutuality is achieved
which can in turn become a dynamic for social change. I am
aware of the dissensions and disillusions which accompany the
women's movement as sadly and sorely as they accompany other
movements. However, I see that potentially dissension can
become a means for further understanding; that disillusion-
ment can become the creative urge to fashion more realistic
hopes. Some feminists will respond to this potentiality by
making it reality, and the mutuality among women will be
deepened. I dare to think that the deepening of mutuality
can strengthen a group so that the invitation to mutuality

extends beyond the group. As women actualize a mutuality as a group within society, they not only achieve the power to enact new opportunities for women within the society as a whole, but they also bring that mutuality as a value to bear upon society as a whole.

Second, the value of mutuality is actualized within ② society through the very breaking of traditional roles when they are assumed by women. That is, when we break tradition by taking unaccustomed roles, we make it difficult if not impossible for others to relate to us solely in terms of the role. Since we have changed the role, we cannot be masked by the role: we shape it; it does not shape us. This forces those with whom we work to choose between not relating to us at all, or relating in terms of the qualities, talents, and competencies we as persons bring to our work. While, unfortunately, some try to live within the first alternative, nevertheless our work is usually essential to the organization or institution; relationship is required for efficient functioning of the whole. In relating to us as persons, our colleagues find themselves willy-nilly in the realm of mutuality.

Mutuality is also fostered by feminists through the uni- ③ queness of women's presence in society. Whereas, all other oppressed groups may be kept at a social and personal distance from the elite class, with personal relations developed in working situations easily confined to that public sphere, women cannot be so isolated because relationships between women and men are essential to humanity. The encounter between men and women takes place in every sphere of daily living -- home, work, play; all aspects of life reflect the complementary polarities of a humanity which is both male and female. Furthermore, the encounter between women and men/ takes place in every class and group -- our presence cuts across distinctions of race, wealth, politics, religion. The

implication of our pervasive presence in society is that as
we achieve identities we ourselves forge in openness and mutuality, these values will be pressed into every arena of
life. The ramifications extend from the personal sphere,
wherein release from domination must touch the deepest relationships, to the social sphere, where dominating structures
of hierarchically-ordered society must be brought deeply into
question. The value of mutuality stresses relationships
based upon personhood to the mutual enrichment of each person;
this value holds catalytic potential for restructuring both
personal and social living.

I have described some of the ways feminists give concrete form to the values of openness and mutuality in the
struggle toward a more just society. While feminists act
from a feminist ethic which is not necessarily derived from
process philosophy, nevertheless this feminist ethic is so
consonant with process philosophy that in actualizing these
values, feminists are also giving concrete form to process
values. Furthermore, feminists are absolutely necessary for
actualizing process values in society -- as, indeed, is every
oppressed group. That is, if process thinkers wish to see
process values applied in the realm of social justice, they
must depend upon feminists and other oppressed peoples for a
large part of this achievement.

My reason for stressing this dependence is simply the
difference between possibility and actuality, between rhetoric and reality. To talk of values is not yet to achieve them
To know a value as a possibility is important, but it is not
yet a concretely realized value. Openness and mutuality will
not find actualization in our society until we see restricted
groups acting upon an enlarged world of possibilities, until
we see persons as more important than roles, until we see a
deeper bonding of unity enriching the diversity of society.
Unless oppressed groups find a new freedom in society and act
upon it, there is no realization of those values. The proces

of bringing these values about depends upon the result for
its reality. Realizing a process ethic of openness and mutuality depends upon oppressed groups; realizing a process
ethic therefore depends inescapably upon women. Feminist
action is not something process thinkers can do without in
the field of ethical change. To put it even more strongly,
without feminist action, the process ethic cannot possibly
be extended into the whole of society.

I began this paper by noting that both process and feminist thought unite in my own experience. Let me conclude,
then, by simply pointing out that the positions I have outlined are not theoretical for me, but existential. The process conceptuality has revitalized my worship of God, and illumined my relationships. My sense that God calls me to
openness and transformation gives me confidence and hope in
times when I otherwise feel little ground for either. Regarding my comments on feminist ethics, I am now an assistant
professor of theology in a school where that position has
never before been held by a woman. I find my transformation
of the role has indeed fostered interactions whereby my colleagues relate to me as the person I am; expectations are
held in abeyance, since it is uncertain now as to which expectations do or do not fit the case of a woman teaching theology. This sense of newness appears to foster a new ground
for mutuality within my seminary community.
I well realize the effectiveness of my suggestions in my
own experience in no sense makes them normative, nor frees
others from possible conceptual problems or overly idealistic
hopes. I am myself a feminist continuously in process; I
must continually test ideas and practice. It belongs to the
joy of both feminist and process experience that such testing
does not threaten, but instead opens the possibility of creative transformation into a new future.

NOTES

[1]Alfred North Whitehead, *Process and Reality* (Corrected Edition). New York: The Free Press, 1978.

[2]*Ibid.*, 345-51.

[3]*Ibid.*, 345f.

[4]The suggestions given here are complex, and require a fuller argument in terms of process metaphysics. I have attempted this in "The Question of Immortality," *Journal of Religion* (57/3) July, 1977.

THE DYNAMICS OF FEMALE EXPERIENCE:

PROCESS MODELS AND HUMAN VALUES

PENELOPE WASHBOURN

A temptation in approaching the relation between feminism and process thought is either to compare them, or to contrast them, or to say what each can learn from the other, or to show how feminists are really process thinkers, or that all process thinkers are "closet" feminists: I would like to avoid this approach and begin strictly confessionally and tell the story of the association of two themes in my own intellectual development. I am grateful for the opportunity to examine these two areas of thought systematically, since I have been holding them together in my own mind in a rather unsystematic manner for several years.

It was process thought that taught me to be a feminist, certainly it was process thought that taught me to be interested in questions concerning women and religion. Perhaps I could say now in retrospect that my being drawn to the study and development of a process mode of thinking may also have been related to an unconscious awareness that it offered me not only a more viable theological and philosophical framework than any other, but also an opportunity to integrate my identity as a woman within a religious framework.

These concerns were quite below the level of conscious awareness both on my part and by my teachers in process

thought when I began my studies. My first attempt to associate the two areas of thought was for a conference on women
and the church at the Cathedral of St. John the Divine in New
York in 1971. My paper rather surprised my theological mentor, Daniel Day Williams. I had suggested that there was a
relationship between models of God, particularly Hartshorne's
dipolar concept of God and a feminine aspect of God. In "Re-
discovering the Feminine in God" I had proposed that
Whitehead and Harshorne's view that every event, including
God, has an abstract or fixed element and a dynamic or relational aspect, was also an appropriate manner in which to
conceive of a masculine and feminine aspect of an event. The
"dipolarity" of God meant that the traditional description of
God as Absolute, Infinite, Omnipotent, Perfect, represented
only one aspect of God. God's concrete nature for process
thinkers is God in relationship, creative, loving, suffering,
changing, affected by the world. Process philosophers and
theologians contrast the abstract definition of God's essential nature received from the scholastic philosophical tradition with the Biblical picture of God's dynamic interaction
with the historical events of his people.

I thought in 1971 that there was a connection between
the emphasis in process theology on the dipolar concept of
God's nature and our need to rediscover the feminine aspect
of God and theology. I suggested that there was a parallel
between the concrete nature of God and the feminine aspect of
God as expressed, for example, in the Biblical Wisdom litera-
ture.

Neither Whitehead nor Hartshorne themselves suggested
that one could make the identification abstract = masculine,
concrete = feminine, and I am not sure that I would attempt
that simplistic division today. Nevertheless, I was a process theologian *before* I became aware of the possibilities
of a feminist theology. For me, studying process philosophy

and theology was the "radicalizing" experience which led me
into feminist questions concerning the other limitations of
our religious conceptual categories.

In thinking about the issue of the dipolar nature of God
today it is evident that the identification of the two aspects
of God's nature with masculine and feminine is incorrect. For
Hartshorne the abstract is included *by* the concrete nature,
not the other way around. The character, the timeless, fixed,
static absolute aspect of anything is *a part of* the dynamic,
concrete, changing social reality. In that sense, existentially speaking, the concrete nature is more inclusive, has
priority in terms of our knowledge of God, since it is through
the concrete nature that we appreciate what is timeless or
essential to God's nature.

It would be foolish to suggest that the "feminine" has
priority over the "masculine" elements of life, nor would I
today defend a definition of "feminine" and "masculine" which
emphasized the stereotypical definition of masculine as the
ordering, structuring and rational aspect of life, while assigning the feminine to the creative, dynamic, feeling and
mysterious aspects. Even as abstractions the term "feminine"
and "masculine" are problematic since they reflect cultural
values and are not "essences" in themselves. As we know from
the study of imagery surrounding the Great Goddesses of
Babylon and Egypt, the concept of law and order and structure
are associated with her rule of the heavens and are not the
exclusive properties of a male image of deity.

It is primarily process theology's criticism of the static, hierarchical ordering of society and an image of the absolute power of God that I found helpful for a feminist critique of theology and social order. Feminist thought shares
with process philosophy and theology an understanding of the
need to revise the fundamental categories of the Western tradition. It has been with great delight that I have discovered

in more recent years that the earliest feminists also saw
that any change in women's role in society would involve a
similar shift in fundamental religious presuppositions.

Mary Wollstonecraft, writing in 1792 in the atmosphere
of the French Revolution saw clearly the effects of absolute
hierarchical power in all levels of government in relation to
women's role in society. In the *Vindication of the Rights of
Woman* she states that every profession in which great subordination of rank constitutes its power, "is highly injurious
to morality."[1] In her view the army and the clergy are
equally destructive. Monarchical and priestly power foster
a chain of subordination, command and despotism. For her "it
is the pestiferous purple which renders the progress of civilization a curse!"[2]

Most significantly, Wollstonecraft saw that it was adu-
lation of God's nature as all powerful, which was the cause
and justification for the injustice in human social order and
morality as it existed in her time. For her, a new view of
God's power would be necessary to change the structures of
society and the subjugation of women to male authority.

> The only solid foundation for morality appears to
> be the character of the supreme Being; the harmony
> of which arises from a balance of attributes; --
> and, to speak with reverence, one attribute seems
> to imply the *necessity* of another. He must be just,
> because he is wise; he must be good, because he is
> omnipotent. For to exalt one attribute at the ex-
> pense of the other equally noble and necessary,
> bears the stamp of the warped reason of man -- the
> homage of passion. Man, accustomed to bow down in
> power in his savage state, can seldom divest him-
> self of this barbarous prejudice, even when civili-
> zation determines how much superior mental is to
> bodily strength; and his reason is clouded by these
> crude opinions, even when he thinks of the Deity.
> His omnipotence is made to swallow up, or preside
> over his other attributes, and those mortals are
> supposed to limit his power irreverently, who think
> that it must be regulated by his wisdom.[3]

For Mary Wollstonecraft the issue concerning women's social role was one of the relation of power to justice. Absolute power leads necessarily to injustice. I find her awareness most significant that a change in woman's role in society needs to involve a change in the theological imagery. It suggests that feminism and process thoguht have indeed a common genesis in the history of ideas, in the intellectual, political, theological and social ferment in Europe of the 17th and 18th centuries. (This point can also be demonstrated by looking at Leibniz's society of monads.)

On the American scene, it is also remarkable that the early women suffragists in the mid-nineteenth century, Lucretia Mott, Susan B. Anthony, Elizabeth Cady Stanton, etc., came from non-traditional religious groups, Quakers and "free-thinkers!" Changes in theological imagery and religious structure and order provided them with a basis for action concerning women's role in the political order. It is evident to me, without trying to prove any strict interrelationship, that the forces which influenced the development of process thought, evident in the writings in Leibniz, Hegel, William James and others, were the same that produced the feminist critique of society. A dedication to process rather than stasis, to egalitarian structures of social order rather than monarchial ones, an openness to the future, a critique of concepts of absolute power and authority, a new view of interrelationships; these are common feminist and process themes. It is no accident that the man whose thought inspired the most significant political revolution in our time, Karl Marx, read Hegel and was also inspired by evolutionist Charles Darwin's "Origin of the Species" to the extent that he dedicated a book to him. Marx's critique of the subjugation of woman, of the meaning of marriage and the patriarchal family, was perhaps not foreseen by either Hegel or indeed by Charles

Darwin, though we can now see that he carried the process
aspect of their thought through to its ultimate implications
for women's role in society.

I

   Process thought can, I believe, contribute much to feminist thinkers and concerns, particularly in terms of a dynamic and organic model of experience. Process thought can not
only provide a framework for a richer understanding of human
experience for feminists but more specifically it can add a
new dimension to the analysis of female experience.
   One of the most fundamental problems in contemporary
feminist writing both within the field of religion and outside of it, lies in the definition of what it means to be female. The debate centers around the significance of distinctive body experience and female sexuality for our understanding of women. To suggest that body experience, including its
procreative function, bears a significant relationship to female identity, appears to many feminists to be a reactionary
move, serving only to subtlely reintroduce 'motherhood, apple
pie' and so-called "feminine" characteristics.
   This is a problem that exercises me profoundly. Is there
anything specific, unique and distinctive to female experience that is affected not by her socialization but by the
quality of her body experience? What is the meaning of this
'difference' if indeed there is one? How can men and women
be declared to be both equal and different? What is the relationship of body experience to identity, are there any such
things as 'feminine' characteristics? All these are explo-
sive questions.

In recent years there has been a change in certain aspects of feminist concerns. While the major emphasis on changing the political order for women has not abated, another theme has emerged. The question that is now raised concerns our very values themselves. To what extent has the very ideal of humanness to which the newly liberated woman aspires has been based on a male model which excludes valuable aspects of human behaviour so long associated with women that they are labelled 'feminine' and thus negated by men and feminists alike? Under this category of 'feminine' behavior of course were often included the traditional behaviours of conceiving, bearing, nursing and caring for children, and the less aggressive or active qualities, the more "internal" viewpoint of womankind.

It is women writers, artists, essayists, poets and painters who have been the forerunners in the recent attempts to integrate all aspects of female sexuality into a new view of woman in society. In this area I believe process modes of thought can be most useful in healing what appears a division in feminist thought over the meaning of body experience to the person. Feminist thinking needs to embrace with more vigor not only a critique of absolute power and authority and hierarchial social structures, but also a new understanding of experience. Process thought is particularly valuable for feminists because it proposes an organic view of social order. The distinctiveness of this perception lies in seeing the ultimate elements of reality as events which are a specific "coming together" in time of elements of previous events. The particular network of social relationships is termed a "society" by Whitehead. By defining the essence of reality as social the process thinkers are saying that there is no such thing as isolated individuality. We "take in" the reality of others who have already achieved determinancy in the process of becoming a defined event.

I am at this point liable to criticism by process thinkers because I am using my own terms to express what is usually technically expressed in the special language of Whiteheadian philosophy. However, technical jargon very often obscures what I believe are very clear ideas, so I am prepared to take that risk.

The genius of a process view of the self is that it emphasizes not the distinction of the mind from the body but the network of interrelationship between the events and societies of events "in their neighborhood", so to speak. To be organically related is to be growing, interdependent, emergent from and responsive towards other events. The stress is on the living of unity of individuals. There are tissues of connections between distinctive events. It is hard to know where one "individual" begins and the other ends.

I may be giving the impression that Whitehead and Hartshorne are monists in that everything is one. The balance between subjectivity and the achievement of individual value with interdependence is a delicate one. Because of the processive character of events there is a newness, a spark of creativity and individuality and thus value, even in the context of emphasis on the fact that we take into ourselves aspects of the achieved value of other events.

Perhaps a good example of this approach lies in examining the social nature of ideas and thoughts. Each new idea is part of a complex series of interrelationships of other thoughts, the words of others and of course my own previous thoughts and the bio-chemical processes involved. A Whiteheadian perspective on the nature of thought preserves its social and interactional aspect and yet maintains the uniqueness of each fresh insight.

In process thought there is no 'me' apart from my body. The idea that we are souls or rational minds inhabiting bodies is completely dispelled by a process way of thinking

and offers us the possibility for not only understanding our
relationship to others "outside" our own bodily unities, but
to the "others" that make up our inner events. In the organic
model of the self the absolute distinctions between physical
and mental or spiritual self and others breaks down. The organic model of the self and the distinctive mode of viewing
personal identity and its relation to others offered by process categories can, I believe, contribute depth to a feminist discussion of what is human and what is distinctive about
female experience.

II

My major concern, these past several years, has been my
body. As a participant in a physical process called conception, pregnancy, labor, expulsion, lactation, and a continuing participant in a process called menstruation and coitus,
I have continually asked myself, "what does going through all
these events have to do with my perceptions about reality?
Does my experience in these actions point to something specifically female? How does that relate to *my* theology, sym-
bology and to the meaning of my own human experience? How
can I integrate my physical experiences with the religious
tradition in which I was raised? How do they relate to non-
procreative females or those in different cultural situations?
Are they spiritual events of a new quality? Since the work
of Margaret Mead we must indeed be careful to make *any* cross-
cultural assumptions about any so-called typical "feminine"
behaviour associated with female body events.

Process thought has taught me to be concerned about the
body. I suspect that my concern is also an awareness that
process thinkers themselves, such as my own mentor Daniel Day
Williams in *The Spirit and Forms of Love*, fail finally to

deal adequately with sexuality. It is my conviction that
feminist issues both in religion and in politics or economics
center around the value and meaning ascribed to female body
experience by men and by women themselves. Early feminist
thought was naive in its thinking that for women or men sexuality made no difference, it was the "person" that counted.
Mary Wollstonecraft idealized a society when pure reason
would prevail. Process models of thought have shown us that
any simple dichotomy between mind and body can be avoided.
If one accepts the view that there is no division between the
so-called mental and the so-called physical events then one's
view of the self is radically changed. Rather than there
being a "me" who is affected by the so-called physical events
of my body, there are series of events with physical and
mental aspects each interrelated in social order with other
"events". My thoughts, feelings, emotions, the "brain"
events, are interconnected, parts of other events, both those
"within" my so-called body space and those "outside" it.
Those outside events are the neighborhood, so to speak. They
are the immediate physical and social context of the society
of my own body. The view of "self-hood" as a continually
changing yet a "presiding" social order taking its new identity from the many events of its own "body", is, I believe,
of immense value in a discussion of the specific nature and
effect of female sexuality. Women cannot divorce themselves
from their own body experiences. One of the by-products of
both the patriarchal and mechanistic views of the self is
that men and women have been alienated from their own sexual
processes.

     While there has been a certain "transcendentalist" ten-
dency in modern feminist criticism and a desire to overcome
the limitation of "carnal" existence (as in the work of
Simone de Beauvoir), I believe a more fruitful approach is

to challenge the mind/body dichotomy. To appreciate the
significance of the events of female sexuality freed from
this mind/body dualism opens up new possibilities for women
and men alike. Since women have perhaps been less successful
in disassociating themselves from their body experiences
(they were traditionally perceived as more connected to the
earth), it is possibly women who can experience at first hand
the sense of organic unity of distinctive body processes and
their harmony and interrelationships.

Women are able (as indeed are men in parallel ways) to
experience the sense of this organic model of self advocated
by process thought in a vivid manner distinctive to their own
body structure. In experiencing the particular patterns of
menstruation, intercourse, orgasm, conception, pregnancy,
birth, lactation and menopause, the traditional view of the
self as a soul or mind within a body begins to collapse.
There are several elements to this new awareness.

First, the self/other distinction is eroded in female
experience. For example, the idea of "oneself" as having absolute boundaries can no longer be sustained in pregnancy.
"I" am the "other" the "other" is "me". Viewing the fetus
as a parasite on the mother's body maintained the idea of
the separate selves. In all recent research on pregnancy the
dramatic interrelationship between fetus and mother is demonstrated and the use of any drugs, even an aspirin, can be
detrimental to the fetus. Process thinkers are fond of
quoting Paul's "I am in you and you are in me and we are all
one body". There is no human experience, not even coitus, as
able as pregnancy to illustrate what is often obscured by our
apparent separateness; we are essentially interrelated to one
another, to the events of our "own" bodies and to outside
events.

Second, the distinction between body and mind is chal-
lenged by women's experience. The events of female sexuality

powerfully suggest that there can be no simple breakdown between physical and emotional, social conditioning and personal feeling, "what my body is doing" and "what I am doing
to my body". How do I influence my body experiences, how do
my experiences in turn influence my attitudes, these become
circular questions from which there is no escape. The chem-
istry and physiology is not one thing and me and my feelings
and my cultural conditioning, another. The medical model implicitly assumes this division and women have been notori-
ously treated at the hands of this profession. To see every
event as having a physical and a mental pole frees one ultimately from having to make a decision about things that are
"merely" physical or sensations, and things that are "just in
your mind". To accept an organic view of the self involves
letting go of this artificial dichotomy which presumed to
make a distinction between mind and body. Approaching the
body wholistically would involve viewing the aspects not as
differeing functions but as a series of processes with inter-
connections.

For the organic view of the self there is neither a
strict determinism of the "body" doing this or that, nor is
the role of emotions and attitudes overplayed to the extent
of complete subjectivity. As we now discover in recent research, the process thinkers were correct when they suggested
that the mind/body dualism was a fundamental error. Attitudes
to childbirth affect the quality of the experience, the length
of labour and the mortality rate. Nothing is just "in the
mind" particularly not fear and ignorance, they have evident
and dramatic "physical" counterparts. The interrelationship
goes the other way too; moods, depression, elation have chemical components. The foods we eat, the coffee we drink, affect what we "are". Depression and stress have evident
"physical effects".

Participating in the specific elements of female sexuality involves, then, a significant confirmation of a process view of the self, the organic relatedness of all events, the dissolution of absolute boundaries between self and other and the denial of simplistic divisions between physical and mental aspects of the self.

Third, the meaning of time is changed for women. The most evident characteristic of female body experience which confirms process models, is the changed concept of time that women can experience because of the patterns of their own sexual structures. The action of tearing down, of renewing, the continual transformation of the body through its menstrual cycle, through all of its sexual phases including pregnancy, birth and lactation and menopause is evidence of a continuously changing reality, not a fixed one. My body is not one entity but many, continually in development, becoming, moving from one phase to the next. It is this constant reminder of the flow (excuse the pun) of life through the sexual experiences that has made the female body seem weak and dependent to our Christian culture. To be "subject" to patterns and processes of "so-called" "lower" orders has and is still seen as a burden, an inconvenience in a culture based on presuppositions of man's rational control over his environment, including his own body. Women too have suffered from this concept of the self and are still under its power as is shown by the increasing use of methods to artificially induced labor at a "time" convenient for the doctor and the patient, rather than be "subject to" the inner time of the organism's own development and readiness for labor. The a alienation of women from their own bodies, their distrust and fear of the processes of their sexuality in all its forms are the result of this view of the self, still typical of the medical profession, that sees the body as an object to be controlled, used and manipulated rather than to be cooperated with.

Being able to find value in *all* processes of female sexuality, not only in those evidently associated with pleasure,
involves, I believe, coming into contact with the body's
rhythms; accepting the growth and development and resolution
of different phases. Being "subject" to the body is part of
this participation. The fear in childbirth is that we are
"out of control". It is indeed the experience of being "out
of control" that is the possibility of full orgasmic satisfaction as well the possibility for allowing the processes of
labor to do their work with minimum hindrance. Accepting the
inner time, the seasons of the body, will give women maximum
enjoyment of their sexuality.

                                III

Finding a new model for our view of the self and the
body remains an essential task for feminists. Process thought
can provide us with an understanding both of the dynamic
character of human experience and also of its organic nature.
What more dramatic action than the events of female sexuality!
Something new comes into being, something, a previous state,
is lost. A woman's body is a history of major events: the
beginning of menstruation, first intercourse, conception,
miscarriage, pregnancy, birth, lactation, menopause: begin-
nings and endings; radical shifts in shape, size, form. Each
phase builds, takes from the last, and yet is new and distinctive. No one menstrual period is the same as the previous.

In a woman's body the tragic aspect of life is also dra-
matically experienced. Each action opens up some possibilities and closes others forever. Process thought clearly defines that there will be the loss of some values as soon as
any possibility is actualized. The actualization of some

values is dependent on the loss of some other values perman-
ently. Nowhere is this more true than in the events of female sexuality. To menstruate opens up a new future but involves the loss of childhood. The first intercourse is the
end of a previous state of knowledge and experience. Once
pregnancy is established the body is changed, irrevocably.
If a pregnancy terminates, either by spontaneous or thera-
peutic abortion, that possibility is gone. Choosing to procreate or not to procreate, to end one's fertility or,
through cessation of birth control, to begin it, each decision and event closes off a range of possible experiences
and opens up others. This mixture of gladness and sadness,
of regret and thankfulness is typical whatever form of
choices are actualized. I find this aspect of process
thought very helpful in dealing with what one might call the
tragic elements of life and of female experience. The breasts
that were sucked will never be the same. The skin that was
stretched will never return to its previous state. Value is
only achieved at a price, the loss of other values: there is
no going backwards. Perhaps it is through the acceptance of
this basic process perspective on the necessary loss in life,
that women can cease to feel the need to apologize for or
hide their pain or regret for the possibilities that are
closed forever in their own bodies. Perhaps we can cease
trying to find *one* model for female existence but recognize
that whatever possibilities become actualized some values
will be gained, others lost. The choices are made in each
moment; we experience the ongoingness of creativity and yet
know that loss is real even within the overall creative
action of life.

In choosing the events of female sexuality as a way to
reflect on the organic and process nature of our experience
I have not meant to be prescriptive about the nature of female fulfilment. I have tried to suggest that those of us

who experience reality embodied in femaleness and its cycles
of fertility have a particular avenue to a metaphysical perspective on the nature of reality. The interesting point is
that none of these events are *necessarily* "felt" as fulfilling, nor as carrying the implications that I suggest. Apart
from the fact that the female body undergoes dramatic changes
each month, goes from being pre-menstrual to menstrual to
menopausal, there is nothing necessary in the way that is experienced. We are "social" bodies: the manner in which the
so-called events inside my body are experienced is affected
by a variety of factors, both chemical and psychological,
cultural and personal. One of the most helpful elements of
Whiteheadian thought in this regard is, I believe, in being
able to see that there are physical and mental poles to each
event. The cultural conditioning is embodied in the way in
which I experience menstruation, whether or not I achieve orgasm, and how my body responds to menopause.

                                   IV

     Another question is what the model of female fulfilment
might be for the non-productive woman or post-reproductive
woman. What about those who choose not to actualize the reproductive or lactative or orgasmic possibilities in their
own bodies? Are they fulfilling their bodily potential? I
think the answer to this lies not in a simple statement but
in a further question about the quality of any event as experienced and its relationship to the whole. As in any sexual experience there is an enormous range for possible response. The question might be, have I allowed myself to be
changed by the actions of my body, have the actions of the
one aspect been enhanced and supported by the whole, and in
turn enriched and added value to the whole? It is not just

a question of whether or not I was pregnant, but whether the potentialities of this body being pregnant in my own personal and social context were able to be actualized. This is Whitehead's point about the achievement of value that *in the situation* the maximum good in the selection of possibilities might be achieved. Being pregnant is not an isolated event, it is an event in the world, both of my body and the social world. Choosing to actualize the possibility of pregnancy involves more than biological satisfaction, it relates to the potential for being pregnant in the world at hand. My environment is therefore not only the "inner" environment of my body but the "outer" environment of my social situation, my human community as well as my physical community.

That is why it is so important for the outer and inner context to be supportive to the new events. Sex can be a desultory or mechanical event. It can also be a life-transforming total response of the whole organism in which every cell feels the effect. A mother who nurses her child out of a sense of duty will transmit her anger by lessening her own milk supply. The menopausal changes of the body can be experienced as the symptoms of the loss of identity, as they are too frequently in our own society. In societies where women gain status as they grow older, where they have a significant role to play, as in some non-western societies, the "menopause" as we know it with its attendant physical and psychological sufferings does not exist as a major life crisis for the woman.

The fulfilment of the individual woman or man is not in the mere fact of putting oneself through an experience. It is the manner in which that event is in harmony with the other events in its neighborhood and enhances their good. it is foolish to suggest that all should actualize the same potentials, since in terms of fertility it is not just an inner event of conception that is significant but its place as an

event in a wider network of meaning. To conceive may bring
joy, or as we know, be the occasion for deep distress and
anxiety when the social community of events is not supportive.

I think the elements of freedom, responsibility and risk
come into play in terms of allowing the actions of our female sexuality to be life-enhancing to the whole body and
"others". The value of female sexuality lies in its ability
to give pleasure. "Pleasure" is involved when the body works
well in "inner" and "outer" harmony, though perhaps I mean
something rather deeper by the term "pleasure" than popular
connotations would suggest. I believe pleasure is fulfilment
at a very fundamental level, though pleasure cannot simply be
defined as "that which feels good." The real meaning of
pleasure is "that which gives joy," and in many cases the
boundary line between "pleasure" and "pain" are narrow indeed.
The grimaces on the face of woman in ecstacy on the verge of
orgasm may be compared to the straining and groaning in the
face of the woman pushing out her child at birth. The one we
usually call pleasure and the other pain. In truth, they are
similar and when the effort is over the total body is at
peace.

"Pleasure" is what floods back into the whole body as
each event is experienced working in its fullness. Just as
runners who exercise their muscles experience the pleasure
and pain of feeling their muscles work, so in all other
aspects of the body we feel good or receive joy when we are
able to feel the actions of one part of the body enhancing
the rest. Giving value to the rest of the body, to others
in the immediate society is, as Whitehead suggested, our contribution to immortality. What a large responsibility we
have to discover what the needs are of the individual processes in the society of our body to enhance the futures of
other bodily events. Brain cells need to think, muscles
need to be exercised, the blood needs oxygen. As women and

men our very lifestyle and cultural conditioning interfere
not only with the processes of sexuality but with many other
life processes. To be healthy is to be life-enhancing and to
contribute value to others.

This is where a faith dimension comes in -- not only in
terms of women's attitude to their own experience but in its
relationship to the whole. The cosmology of the western intellectual tradition saw spirit and body as two separate entities. Only in the new metaphysical framework of process
thought can the spiritual and the material be seen as aspects
of one reality. Those who suffered most tragically under the
previous Christian framework were women who were relegated to
the realm of the body with a loss of spiritual identity.
Sometimes they strove for acceptance by denying their lesser
part and achieved spiritual parity with men (almost!) at the
price of disowning their own sexuality. The new feminism of
our time may now embrace a new view of the self as an organic
whole. We can find spiritual value in bodily experience not
because they are redeemed or justified according to some divine plan or purpose, but because ultimate value is found as
a characteristic of each individual event. The spiritual
significance of the events of female body experience lie in
their value and joy for others, both for my "own" future
events and those in my immediate environment. Women have
been taught to believe that their bodies and their sexuality
if not evil, are certainly irrelevant to what is meant by
Ultimate Truth. If the physical has a spiritual dimension,
then perhaps we can follow through with Charles Hartshorne's
suggestion that the spiritual also has a physical dimension.
To say, as he did, that the world is God's "body", would affirm that female sexuality is also part of God's body. The
mystic Julian of Norwich in the 12th century was ahead of her
time when she described God in language of the nursing mother,
though perhaps we may now speak of aspects of all human experience in the language of ultimacy.

V

Until our wider social processes, our ideas, institutions, medical practices and social norms become supportive towards women experiencing value in their bodily events, we will continue to see a destruction of hope for the whole community. The acknowledgement of the existence of women's sexual feelings at the turn of the century was a major achievement and put to flight a host of "feminine" disorders such as "hysteria" and the "vapours." Bitterness, resentment and physical exhaustion were the result of women being trapped into procreative behaviour. The advent of birth control, while by no means a fully satisfactory achievement in its present state, was the opportunity for women to experience procreation not as an obligation but as a choice. There is still so much to be done in the wider social arena, in law and social policy, to release women from the drudgery of work and from all forms of mental and social constriction. The feminist revolution is at its most fundamental a revolution that will involve the whole social fabric and our view of the human organism and its place within the fuller social order.

By paying attention to the needs of their own bodies for health women will indeed focus on elements that are essential for all forms of creative transformation. The principles by which we govern our lives, particularly in western industrialized society, are antithetical not only to human life or female bodily fulfilment but also to the processes of life on the non-human level. To be able to see the universe as a community of interrelated processes is one of the most essential of modern tasks. An organic view of the self is the basis for an organic view of the universe. It is in this sense that the ecological movement and feminist concerns are both expressive of a world perspective that is common to "process thinkers." I think that women are able to be particularly sensitive to these new directions, since they have been so largely alienated from the dominant patriarchal mode of thought and order.

To accept that human experiences may be different between the sexes and yet equally valid is one of the most difficult of human problems. By paying attention to the dynamic nature of their own sexual patterns, to the quality of interrelatedness of their particular female sexual experience and to the psycho-somatic unity of the self, women can enhance our understanding of human experience as a whole. The exclusion of women from the public domain and the negation of their perceptions resulted in an atrophied and disembodied view of the self. Acutely aware of changes in themselves, women can make concrete William James' and the Buddhist perception that each of us is *many* selves, fixed as far as the past is concerned, open to a new state in the future. This process orientation can be an encouragement to women who despair that their socialization, their history or their bodies condemn them irrevocably to a certain course of action. The past limits and suggests boundaries but never determines the future. Actualizing our potential within general limits remains our task. For women it means actualizing and maximizing the possibilities within the general context of a female body structure. Whatever value that particular experience has to oneself and to society, whatever meaning, significance and quality whose events will have, is a matter not of the living out of a foreordained "female destiny", but the free actions of all the events that go to making up the society of my own body.

Reaffirming the indeterminate nature of existence as process thought does, is an act of faith as fundamental as the affirmation that process is ultimately creative not destructive. Feminists have faith too, that women have an ultimate significance and contribution to life as a whole

because, and not "in spite of", their experiences as women.
Valuing their distinctiveness in no way claims superiority
to men's experience. What it *does* claim is that an understanding of the dynamics of female experience is an important
aspect of any redefinition of personal and social order and a
description of the value of human experience.

To deny the dominance of human against the "non-human"
environment or of mind over matter is a major element of an
organic and social view of reality. It is this dominance of
mind over matter and human over non-human that encourages us
to treat our bodies as if they were machines, our physical
environment as if it were inert or to be plundered and used
up for our benefit. By not perceiving the interrelatedness
of all things we are well on the way to a major tragedy in
human civilization.

To let go an attitude of dominance implies an openness
to learn, a humility, a quality of listening to the wider
social environment. We need to pay attention to the parti-
cularity of bodily processes, to rest when rest is needed,
to exercise, to stimulate or to relax, not according to a
man-made "work-plan" but when the time is right. We must
"listen" to our bodies.

This view of the flow of time will shake the very basis
of modern order. Clock time is not human time and our very
patterns of daily activity, of work and leisure, follow an
efficiency model rather than one which takes account of the
processive nature of time. Under challenge is our narrowly
scientific and technological method of solving problems; one
that tends to see reality and humans as merely chemical processes, devoid of any of the subjective, emotional or value-
laden aspects of life.

The dynamics of female sexuality are similar to those of
all other events at some level. As women bear witness to
their own experience they will be speaking of life processes

which are of value to the whole of the universal community.
Process thought and feminism can be beneficial to each other.
Process philosophy can aid feminism by providing a wider conceptual model for social existence. Feminism, while pursuing
its own goals, can critique process theology for its own ab-
stractionist tendencies and speak to the vitality of sexu-
alized experience in our search for an understanding of ultimate value in life.

NOTES

[1] Mary Wollstonecraft, *Vindication of the Rights of Woman*
(New York: W. W. Norton, 1967), 45.

[2] *Ibid.*, 47.

[3] *Ibid.*, 84f.

BECOMING HUMAN:

A CONTEXTUAL APPROACH TO DECISIONS ABOUT

PREGNANCY AND ABORTION

JEAN LAMBERT

Moral and ethical discussion about abortion is a raw
wound in the body of human interpretation. To this wound,
feminists and process thinkers may apply healing reason. To
do so, we need to claim both the shared and the particular
resources of our intellectual perspectives.

We must emphasize the value to human becoming of our
capacity for choosing and accepting. Human life requires
both. To explain the role of these emphases in contemporary
discussions of pregnancy and abortion requires interpreting
the process of becoming human.

In my personal and intellectual history two movements
intertwine: questing and being called. I have experienced
their movements variously as a sequence in which one begins
as the other ceases and as a battle of equals pulling in opposite directions. Rarely, questing and being called have
produced a fugue in which each moves in relation to and mutually defines the other.

Working with these movements has formed a pattern in me
particularly receptive both to feminism and thinking proces-
sively. To me feminism is solidarity with other women in

political criticism and hoping for a new future. By process thought I mean a particular system of conceptual criticism that offers an integrated vision. Both feminism and process thought recognize the dynamics of creative action. Creation occurs for both when an individual's inner impulse finds responsive resonance with her society's history and imaginative future. Both inner and outer choose each other and call each other for a common destiny. A woman's urge to grow, to affirm herself, to find her work and do it in the world, harmonizes with her sisters, and their struggle, discovery, encouragement, and challenge become a new system of human action leaving no individual unchanged. Yet, far from blurring individual distinctiveness, such action calls each one to name herself. Sisters increasingly recognize, criticize, and celebrate the identity a woman comes to claim for herself. This is the feminism I have experienced in sisterhood.

Similarly, says Alfred North Whitehead, the most fundamental drops of reality, the events that compose the world are collaborative processes between an individual and the surrounding world. An aim proposed through the subject's past is received, affirmed, and transformed. Call and quest emerge as one, new creature acting its part in a moment of creation. The new creature is then recognized, criticized, and celebrated in the becomings of other creatures, into whose histories it is integrated and through which, though it perishes, it lives forevermore.[1]

Becoming human is both a quest and a response to a call. An individual pursues, takes responsibility, reaches out, grasps. She also finds reality disclosed to her, she is offered, she is grasped, she is accepted, all at the choices of others. Without both, she is not. She is neither pure subject, nor pure object. Becoming human, she loses solitariness and absolute control over her fate. As a woman becomes herself, human society likewise loses its consistency and uniformity, its totalitarian control of its fate. In

reality neither she nor society loses; individuals and society become human together, their existences being interdependent.

An embryo implants in the womb, takes in nourishment,
produces new cells, forms organs and limbs, all according to
genetically prompted impulses toward humanity. Yet, it is
also retained, nourished, cherished, mothered by another,
who chooses to do so. Without both, an embryo is not. It
is neither simply initiator nor simply receiver. Becoming
human it loses its unique status as solitary, independant
cell, genetically controlling its future. And, as embryo becomes human fetus, its mother loses her integrity, becomes
two not one, and loses sole control over her own future. In
reality neither embryo nor mother loses; neither exists without the other. In the moments of conception two quests and
two calls meet: the months of pregnancy and uterine existence,
the moments of birth, and the life spans of mother and offspring, are the struggle and harmony of an intimately interacting society of human becomers. In and between both embryo
and mother choosing and accepting occur together. For both,
conception is a moment of newly becoming human. The embryo
emerges from ranged genetic potentialities as egg and millions
of sperm, into specific potentiality with just these chromo-
somes in these patterns. The mother emerges from ranged potentialities as a woman in myriad relationships into specific
potentiality as bearer of this potential human self. None of
this is sheerly automatic or sheerly deliberate. In each,
givenness and choice meet. A kind of negotiation takes place
Choosing and accepting, questing and being called are moments
in living humanly.

I

These moments of choosing and accepting appear in a conflict that rages within any woman who faces a decision about
continuing or terminating a pregnancy. The conflict between
two equally cherished values appears to trap her. Her regard
for the value of human life as such appears to instruct her
to risk almost any personal loss in order to give the potential child a chance for life. At the same time her regard
for the value of her own life and its development, whose
course must be changed by the fetus within her, appears to
focus her decision on the question, "what is best for me?"
If she limits her interpretation of the situation to this
dilemma, the woman must deal with the philosophy, psychology,
and morality of her decision so that she rejects one option,
and implicitly, one value. Because the conflict between the
values sets up a "stand-off" the woman may feel only an ab-
solutist position allows any decision at all. Oversimplified,
this dilemma is the ongoing debate between so-called pro-life
and pro-abortion positions.[2]

This unrealistically narrows the theoretical approach to
a decision where human life calls for both choosing and accepting. This narrowing accounts for the arbitrariness of
many arguments offered by moral conservatives, population-
control personnel, and feminists. It is the underlying
structure of the irrational climate in which much current
discussion of pregnancy and abortion takes place. Yet, almost
any imaginable pregnancy demands respect both for human life
as such and for the particular individuals' own historical
existences. But a woman cannot do this unless she accounts
for the broader, more complex dimensions of the decision.

The days following the discovery that she is pregnant
are not a time when a woman can realistically begin formal,
dispassionate philosophical and moral inquiry. But she must

decide. With care she may make an informed, sensitive, and
relatively free choice.

Both feminism and process thought contribute strong elements to forming such choices and clarify the context and
meaning of the decision-making process. Feminism as a philosophical perspective -- most compellingly articulated in two
works of Mary Daly[3] -- is still more powerful as an instru-
ment of social and attitudinal criticism than as an integrative vision. Whiteheadian metaphysics offers, on the other
hand, a highly developed vision of the nature of reality.
Therefore, I take as base lines in this discussion of human
becoming themes central to Whitehead's metaphysics. I have
articulated these resources consciously informed by experiences of sisterhood and by methods of feminist analysis.

In such a controversial discussion it is only fair to
acknowledge my convictions. I believe the final decision
about pregnancy must normally be made by the woman. It follows that I also believe women must take primary responsibility for preventing conception and that -- since neither
human planning nor technology is completely reliable -- the
option of a legal, medically competent abortion should be de-
fended for all women. This defense includes financial assistance where necessary. I abhor the carelessness of parents
or women that leads women through ignorance to unplanned
pregnancy, and the violence of specific men and society at
large that oppresses women with unwanted sexual intercourse
that sometimes results in pregnancies. I regret the climate
of rigidity in our culture that penalizes women who decide to
bear children outside marriage. These all reflect our culture's
sexism. At the same time, I believe the decision to abort is
by definition tragic; the possibility of a creative, responsive human being is lost with almost each aborted fetus, and
the particular opportunity for woman to grow and become more
deeply human herself through loving and nurturing a helpless

human infant is lost with each one. Nevertheless, I believe a woman may choose to abort -- aware of the tragedy -- both responsibly and morally.

II

When we decide about pregnancies we express our fundamental convictions about what it means to become human. Four themes within the philosophy of Alfred North Whitehead particularly help develop convictions more thoughtfully: the sociality of individuals; the bodily character of real events; the capacity of events for self-transcendence; and the role of reason in the creativity of the world. These themes are relevant in the becoming of all creatures, but particularly for human becoming.[4]

Individuals are socially related as is characteristic of all reality, including facts both in their internal constitution and in their relations with the world. According to Whitehead, "drops of experience" or "actual occasions" are the final real things, and they come to be and perish in society.[5] They inherit from other occasions which have "decided for them"[6] and they offer their achieved meanings to future occasions for similar incorporation. In this perspective a reality is understandable by analogy to an organism, which inherits from its past, becomes a new thing, and in perishing gives itself to its future. Through its receptivity to its past, an occasion inherits life; through its passivity to the actions of its successors -- after it has perished and is no longer able to act in its own behalf -- a real creature continues to be a contributing factor in the society of fellow creatures. In this rhythm of passage, any reality moves from society to solitariness to society, and from definiteness to vagueness to definiteness. One might equally describe the movement in terms of dominant patterns of relatedness: a

creature emerges from a social matrix, stands alone in its
self-creative phase (which Whitehead calls "concrescence")
and then re-offers itself, in perishing, to its successors
as resource for their processes of becoming.

Finally, though the sociality of the world may thus be
expressed in many ways, it is not the definitive word about
reality, as Whitehead sees it. Though relatedness is univer-
sally characteristic of real things, it does not obliterate
individuals; individuals and society co-create each other.

I spoke about of "drops of experience" and of "actual
occasions." I said that these foundation-components of real
things may be called events. Each event, or drop, must be
understood to have both a physical and a mental aspect. In
any particular event, one aspect may be more apparent than the
other. For example, much that is real is not material, and
for realities such as "the relationship of sight and sound"
or "the relationship of parent and child" the physical nature
of the relation is invisible. For other realities physicality
shows up as a body: a carrot, a lake, a human individual.
Similarly, mentality is not always apparent in real things.
People sometimes give evidence of thinking, but "mentality"
is not limited to us, or to ourselves-when-thinking. Rather,
mentality is the capacity in real things to discriminate or
select relative to aims, and it is observable in this sense
even in inorganic elements. For example, iron filings are
attracted to negative electonic charges, and repulsed by
positive ones. Once attracted, filings and magnet have a
physical relationship, but prior "mentality" in their constituting events makes that relationship possible. An elemental
discrimination is present, and the more complex the body, the
richer its opportunities for mentality.

Within the animal body of a human is a series of experiences which Whitehead calls a centered and "personally ordered
society."[7] This is a kind of "route" of inheritances going
on within, say, myself all the time that inherits in a serial

order from my whole self's experiences and enables the ordering of my activity to goals. My body is the immediate context
for this aspect of my mentality. One way I am human is that I
experience the mentality of the many events of my animal body
not primarily as reflex, intuition, or instinct, but as focus
in a central "coordinator and decider."

Such a conception asserts that neither physicality nor
mentality can exist without the other in any creature. This
amounts to a philosophical doctrine of soul-body interdependence. It does not mean soul-body identity, nor does it mean
simple dominance of either soul or body by the other dimension of its reality. We are wholes, bodied souls and souled
bodies.

Like physicality, the capacity for transcendence, for
being something individual for oneself, is a dimension of all
occasions.[8] It is realized to a high degree in human beings
where, because of a corresponding complex development called
"self", we may speak of self-transcendence. Among even the
elemental occasions transcendence refers also to the continuation of their self-creating influence beyond the limits of
their direct control. Future anticipations contribute to
their self-constituting in the present.

In a sense this capacity starts before an occasion
really begins to exist. The real world of a potential occasion provides an aim which functions for it as a purpose,
luring potentiality into actuality, or -- in theological language -- calling it into being. In becoming actual, the occasion transcends its givens, becoming something new before
it perishes. But in perishing, its transcendent newness sur-
vives and awaits appropriation and participation in the becoming of other occasions.

In Whitehead's language the names given to an occasion's
aim shift as they are applied to the several phases of becoming: initial aim, subjective aim, determinate satisfaction.

These shifts distinguish the aim's relative subjectivity or
objectivity, its potential for directing or for being acted
upon. Through the process by which an occasion comes to be,
the potentials it has inherited come to some specific outcome,
and the "fully determined" aim then ceases to become. As an
achieved meaning it is available for the becoming of other
occasions, and in this availability it transcends the process
that engendered it. Such a process of transcendence goes on
within each cell of a human body and is the coordinating
movement of each whole human self. At the level of conscious
self-reflexive human persons, this capacity for transcendence
may be called spirit as John Cobb puts it.[9] By means of self-
transcendent spirit a human being can look back upon her past,
take responsibility for what she was but has ceased to be,
and anticipate her future, planning or hoping toward what is
not yet.

The fourth theme from process thought is "reason" in the
technical Whiteheadian sense. Whiteheadians understand such
activities as analyzing, discriminating, comparing, and so on,
which we ordinarily associate with "reason," as aspects of
the deeper, more pervasive, richer functioning of the processes of creation. These processes are, themselves, the immediate fountains of reasons, because they engender the actual
occasions, "the only reasons."[10] The occasions are both self
and world-creating, as the processes of concrescence bring
possibilities into new relationships. Abstract possibilities
for structure -- which Whitehead calls "eternal objects" and
which may be thought of as timeless patterns to which the relations among things respond[11] -- are not themselves "reason"
or "reasons." Only real events both purpose and contribute
to constituting other real events and are, as such, the re-
ferents of the term "reason."

In process thought, the human person is interpreted --
at least implicitly -- on the paradigm of the actual occasion. Although it is true that Whitehead's system accounts

for multiple levels of reality and proposes specific terminology and qualifications to refer to them -- including the
human level -- nevertheless any part of reality may be studied
by taking the actual occasion as a kind of paradigm and ap-
plying its phases to analyze the phenomenon in question. This
simplifying procedure may be noted in Whitehead's own work,
as, for example, when he analyzes the development of certain
ideas and discusses the learning process.[12] Applied to human
activity and compared with the specific functions of self-
and world-creation which the actual occasion exhibits, this
procedure suggests that human activity creates both the human
person and the human world.

These four Whiteheadian themes express the nature of
reality and of human becoming. They offer the main bases
that would need to be touched in developing a formal processive doctrine of human beings in the world. Such a doctrine
might illuminate freedom and oppression, responsibility and
dereliction, power and powerlessness, and commitment and individuality which severally define the ways we experience the
dynamism and contradictions of our existence. This chapter's
scope is inadequate for developing all these ideas; however,
these themes sketch my conceptual context for the specific
issues of the decision-making processes connected with pregnancy and abortion.

Two questions must be asked to focus these issues:
(1) what is involved morally in deciding what to do about
pregnancy, and (2) what is involved ethically in the question
whether abortion ought or ought not to be legal? These questions first call for a broader interpretation than an examin-
ation solely of the two "inviolable values" I identified earlier as "rights in conflict." "Bodiedness" is associated
with both the fetus' right to life and the pregnant woman's
right to a high quality of life; both reflect the same value:
individual worth, individual uniqueness, the value of each
and every human life. The specific individual focus,

centered in different bodies, differs. "Life" means something different to a fetus than to an adult woman, for who-
ever they are or may become their interpersonal and intraper-
sonal histories and anticipations are vastly different. Yet
the tension between fetus and pregnant woman does not concern
conflicting values, but the same value -- human life -- which
has specific meaning to each. Or consider individual's
"self-transcendence," which means that the woman's right to
choose is not a different value from the fetus' right to ma-
ture to the point of choosing; rather, the two are applica-
tions of the same value. There is a strange, confusing par-
allelism in these paired relations. The fetus has experienced less life, and therefore might appear entitled to more
of it. The woman has had her integrity violated by an un-
chosen, alien presence within her, and therefore she might
appear deserving of compensatory self-transcendent choice.
These paired relations can cross and re-cross each other with
great complexity, and consequently no simple answer exists to
the puzzles about pregnancy and abortion. Not alone do the
principles of the right to live, the right to choose, or the
reality of human community (expressed in the themes of sociality and reason) account for the relations of mother and fetus. Human life, individual freedom of choice, and human
community must be interpreted with respect for their complex
interrelations.

                               III

     A first reflection on the value of human life signals
that all parties to the discussion about pregnancy and abortion agree the discussion is not about some abstract "value
of life as such" but about the value and rights of human lif
Thus one element in the discussion is a correct concern abou

when human life begins. Despite some popular views, this
question elicits no unambiguous response, either regarding
when a "conceptus" becomes human or what the answer signifies.
    Some ambiguity arises because the discussants cannot
agree on what it is they are differentiating by their varying
beginning-points. The traditional Jewish definition that
human life begins when the newborn draws breath suggests the
capactity for face-to-face interaction within the human community. The traditional Roman Catholic definitions of en-
soulment at conception or quickening, suggest the individuality of the unique human person. A more peculiar ambiguity
arises when we consider that human life characterizes all
living human cells. Each cell bears the genetic code for
some particular human inheritance, whether a sperm, ovum, or
non-reproductive human cell. The work done with cloning of
non-human organisms already suggests some implications of
this genetic fact. If we attempt to reduce the questions
about pregnancy to a matter of simply preserving even human
life, we reach an impasse. How can we decide the graded
value of one cell over another, or of the new cell resulting
from the sperm-ovum combination? Furthermore, the loss of
any cell diminishes the organism, and the loss of many cells
exists continuously as a companion process to producing new
ones. The genetic potentials of all human cells remind us
that the components of the human body are simultaneously of
value to the body they constitute and to potential future
generations of humanity. This places a dual focus and an
ambiguity of meaning within each cell. What of those specialized for reproductive function? Sperm and ova bear this
double meaning, no less than the cells of a finger-tip, which
are specialized far differently. And, the cell resulting
from their fusion likewise "means" both for itself and for
its ever-more-socially-related future, bearing for both self
and others the meanings of its past.

On the most obvious level, this makes human life a continuum; points of transition between phase and phase may be
noted, but these points are always a bit arbitrary to define.

Of more apparent relevance to the present discussion is
an important issue arising from this first reflection: of
what value is the life of the potential offspring of sexual
union? Aspects of the sacred character we traditionally
grant the act of heterosexual intercourse are the drama,
pleasure, and risk of contributing a whole, new member of the
human family. Human societies, including our own, recognize
that more matters in such an encounter than the lives and
energies of the two participants. There is an Other, potentially; even as potential, this Other symbolizes the mysterious creative and reproductive depth of meaning in human intercourse.

Other modes of sexual encounter do not deny this.
Parents of pubescent youth implicitly recognize this dimension in the care they give to their children's behaviour as
they learn to express erotic feelings interpersonally, even-
tually genitally. Homosexual intercourse consciously or unconsciously takes the corresponding risk of creating new persons in the union of the partners, who risk changing and being changed both individually and in partnership into new
persons. Protected heterosexual intercourse also has this
dimension, even though the partners decide against risking
biological conception; Christian marriage services recognize
the potential of the two becoming one flesh, as well as recognizing the potential biological offspring. Even violent,
or exploitative sexual intercourse does not necessarily deny
this symbolic structure so much as rebel against it.

Because conception of new persons in sexual union is
possible, each intercourse entails risk and opportunity for
the whole human community. In the innocent bundle of potentials which may be the biological result of heterosexual

intercourse the deeply creative, as well as reproductive, meaning of human intercourse finds most compelling expression. The fetus is of potential value as the child/adult she or he may become. But even *in utero,* the fetus actualizes value as symbol of "new human being."

Equally relevant in this regard is the value of the particular human life of the woman in whose body such a possibility may grow and the value of the human life of the man whose action has contributed part of its genetic inheritance. These persons have histories and hopes, and they act and respond to the many influences of the world impinging on them every moment. Like the fetus they are valuable to themselves, to each other, and to the whole community.

Moreover, though the lives of both potential parents are to be considered here, the life of the woman requires particular consideration. Not only will her emotional, economic, and social future be affected by her decision about pregnancy, as is also true for the man in question, but her life is directly threatened. Any mother knows the changes she has experienced physically due to her pregnancy; United States mortality statistics document that each 100,000 pregnancies result in 25 maternal deaths.

Out of these three reflections it is possible to draw a provisional summary: By upholding the abstract value of human life we express respect for all persons. In this I agree with the "pro-life" position perspective. Those who defend the rights of the unborn correctly raise the spectre of genetic experimentation, now of growing concern with increased numbers of technicians capable of such research. To erode this respect at any level is to risk eroding it throughout the human spectrum. This also, however, is why "pro-abortion" advocates are correct to ask "what about war?" to the advocates of the "pro-life" position. Both ideologies exaggerate the service of a fundamental commitment. To paraphase John Donne, "Each one's death diminishes me."

A second value to consider is the freedom of individual
human beings. A first reflection here concerns the relation
between such freedom and individual responsibility. A fundamental correlation exists between the possibility of freedom
to choose among alternatives and the condition of human responsibility. Capacity to discriminate among alternatives
and absence of constraints together constitute freedom to
choose. Without both a human cannot properly be deemed responsible for her or his actions. For example, if a mentally
retarded person attacks a public official he suspects of
threatening him, the law may declare the offender unable to
discriminate adequately and elect him not responsible. Only
if he could anticipate the outcomes of his possible actions
could his alternative result from free choice. Or, if an intelligent, healthy adult observes a child drowning fifty feet
away in deep water and, lacking a rope or flotation device,
does not help the child because she cannot swim, that individual may well feel remorse and grief, but is not legally
negligent or guilty of involuntary manslaughter. Such a by-
stander's inability restricted her freedom and thereby her
responsibility. Only if she knew how to swim and observed
the struggling child could she choose freely whether or not
to attempt rescue.

To take responsibility for one's action is to claim the
freedom to choose; to hold another responsible for his or her
actions is legitimate only when he or she is both able and
un-coerced, that is, free to choose among the alternatives.

Having understood this much, we gain understanding of
what freedom of choice may mean for the woman confronting an
unplanned pregnancy. She and society value her freedom of
choice implicitly, at least to the extent to which they value
her being a responsible adult. This applies in turn to all
the persons who may become involved in a decision-making process concerning the pregnancy: the family, the medical personnel, and representatively, the whole society. All have

freedom to choose which somehow enters into the decision. Yet
not all bear equally the burden of the choice. Because the
pregnant woman faces the most severe changes and risks as result of the pregnancy, her freedom and responsibility must,
therefore, be weighed most heavily. Consequently, she ought
to be granted the greatest freedom to choose. And, if such
freedom is denied her, this denial implicitly denies either
her worth or her capacity for responsibility. (Much opposition to abortion "in principle" may reflect less a denial of
women's worth than prejudice against women's capacity to make
responsible decisions.) Yet while hers is the chief responsibility it is not the sole one. In many ways "the community"
participates in her decision.

A further complexity of "individual freedom" concerns
the potential of the fetus to become first an infant, then a
child, and then an adult with her or his own freedom to
choose. *In utero,* and for years after birth, so far as we
can tell, this remains purely potential freedom and responsibility. To the extent to which such a possibility is part of
the "basic equipment" for the human individual -- which post-
Enlightenment societies have assumed -- the fetus must be assumed to "have it potentially." The fetus is not a fully-
human being, but deserves respect as a potential, full participant in the human community. If this is a genuine potential, it must be borne responsibly by society on behalf of the
fetus, and on its own behalf. The burden of such guardian-
ship cannot be taken lightly, though here again it lays on
society no absolute rules.

A third value basic to this discussion is maintaining
and enriching human community. Although individual values
have concerned us to this point, no one is human absolutely
alone. To be human is to be in some form supportive, chal-
lenging community with one's fellows. Aristotle's *Politics*
identifies "the Greek" as "an animal who lives in a *polis*,"

a spatially contiguous, economically and culturally interrelated collection of people whose lives directly co-determine
each other. This tradition continues regardless of the more
individualistic ideology of recent centuries. One process
theologian, Daniel Day Williams, identifies the "image of God"
in human beings -- which, according to Christian theological
interpretation makes us human -- as the "form of creation for
life fulfilled in love" or as our "will to communion."[13]

As we consider questions about pregnancy and abortion in
the wider network of relations in which our humanity finds
definition, we sense the pressures this community exerts on
each venture in decision-making. How shall the decision
take into account the interests of the community, the many
relations through which life may be "fulfilled in love" as
Williams puts it. What about the mother's creativity? Her
social productivity? What about the father's needs and interests? The potential child's? What about society's control over its members? What about the legitimate concern of
society for its continuation and for the quality of its citi-
cenry? What about the advantages to the human spirit of
struggle with difficulties and the discovery of good which
are not immediately apparent? What about the disadvantages
to the human spirit of struggle with difficulties and the
discovery of evils which are not immediately apparent?
Phrases from current developments in the physical and social
sciences evoke the range of issues surrounding the fact that
we value human community: family planning; the population ex-
plosion; eugenics; cloning; sterilization of those with problematic genetic histories. To defend the rights of the community is one way to defend the rights of individuals; it is
not only the exclusive way, but it is one part of the total
picture. Both sides of the individual/communal question must
be remembered. The collective may tyrannize the individual,
and the individual may tyrannize the collective.

Considering these rippling factors, fetus and mother are cast into a fluid situation whose implications are humanly unimaginable. Their extensiveness is owrth mentioning, however, lest we tempt ourselves into fantasizing that a decision about pregnancy can ever be based on knowledge of all the relevant factors and complete foresight about its outcome.

IV

These three values -- human life, individual freedom, human community -- affect our judgment as we reflect on the questions concerning pregnancy and abortion. Strict commitment to any one in isolation from the others will bring one's own decision-making into conflict on the grounds of at least one of the other two. Valuing human life alone, or freedom to choose, or social responsibility, is not adequate. Human life is too complex to reduce to a simple principle or formula. Making a moral decision in an ethical context as complex as this requires, therefore, interpretation of the meaning of these values in their interrelationship. In this task I find particularly helpful the four themes from process philosophy I sketched earlier.

Inasmuch as I am a Christian theologian my approach in these next comments is no doubt further colored and given specific shape by my faith. I would imagine that one such coloration comes from my wish to recognize in the world what Whitehead called the "secular functions" of God, participating with each moment of the world's creative process to contribute direction and save whatever is of value. Based on my process perspective and on my Christian commitment I also tend to rest my moral evaluation less on discrimination and judgment, although these are indispensable, than on action in faith and forgiveness.

My responses to the ambiguities in the questions about pregnancy and abortion come in two stages beginning with some interpretations of the purpose of human life, its course, and the structure of human existence, and drawing on the four processive themes.

My first interpretation issues from a sense of the world in which all types of events and "things" are characterized by analogous processes of self-creation, are socially inter-related, and contribute to the creation of other realities. In such a world the general purpose of any creature is to achieve its own aim in such a way as to contribute to ful-filling the aims of its fellow creatures. This "sense of the world" is informed by deep personal and religious sources, no doubt, but in articulating it I am drawing specifically on Whitehead's metaphysics and particularly those themes I re-ferred to earlier of sociality, transcendence, and reason.

Within this general purposiveness some things are more extensively related and more valuable than others, and there-fore human creatures can be said to have a special place. Some have interpreted Whitehead's description of a hierarchy of societies[14] in such a way that the great complexity of the human being "means" either superior worth or over-arching re-sponsibility. I prefer, however, to recognize the reality of graded value in the world in order to make a different use of it in discussing the purposes of human life. Within my Chris-tian perspective I take this gradation of value discernable in the world to reflect not humankind's intrinsic superior worth, or capacity, but an integrative purpose beyond human grasp and expressed by the term: the aim of God for creation. Within such purpose human life has value granted to it by that inte-grative aim: our lives have the specific value of stewards who are called upon to cooperate with God's aim, caring for the becoming of creatures with tender and intelligent regard, ap-preciating both individual uniqueness and interdependence. Since the integrative purpose of God is, admittedly, beyond

human grasp -- beyond reasonable projection or imagining --
it can only be approximated. Religious persons called "rev-
eletory" certain moments of clear intuition, and I believe
such moments may reveal what cannot otherwise be discerned.
Nevertheless, they are still approximations. Once this qualification is understood, however, one may attempt to describe
God's aim for the world. With other Whiteheadians I would
describe this aim in some such terms as these: it is the increasing of richness of fulfillment and enjoyment for God and
for creatures.

For God and for those who would be stewards of the creation, such an integrative aim implies some resolution of the
conflicts among competing possibilities. Not all potentials
can become actual. All may be entertained and considered,
but some may be harmonized and others must be rejected. This
is not merely a statement about the inevitability of contradictions, but also about the possibilities of richness and
intensity of value; they can be preserved and encouraged only
at a cost. Reducing all competitions to agreements based on
a least common denominator results in blandness and lack of
definition. Therefore the resolution will not be a leveling,
if the aim is toward increased fulfillment and enjoyment;
rather, resolution and reconciliation will mean choices,
either and *or* in opposition, as well as some inclusions; it
will mean real gains and real losses.

For human life the values that constitute life itself
conflict; freedom to choose conflicts with human community;
individual selves conflict with social groups. All choices
entail risks, specifically, the necessity to transgress certain worthy creatures' legitimate rights and certain worthy
possibilities. Any creation involves losing some good; thus
no choice is free of evil. For the loss of good, whether
potential or actual, is evil, in a process perspective, and
it may be evil regardless of its noble motives, its ignorant
provocation, or the greater good it achieves.

I have been raising two factors here: the role of human beings as stewards to achieve the purposes of creation, and the risk attendant on any decision that one may do evil in the course of making the most responsible decision one can make. These factors are crucial in understanding what one is doing in a decision-making process about pregnancy and abortion. We may recognize that both evil and good are likely to result from every decision, and we need not trick ourselves into disregarding one good or calling it evil simply to force ourselves to make some decision at all. We need not take the crude view that the fetus is mere tissue. No, it is potentially a free and responsible human adult. Nor need we take the crude view that the woman is a mere vehicle for the fetus' development. No, she is a free and responsible human adult. The gains for either or both are good; the losses to either or both are evil. Moreover, the dynamic of reality -- that it moves from multiple possibilities, through the narrowing of specific choices, to some determinate outcome -- means that even if we make a choice identical with God's own optimal aim for this moment, the "no" that must accompany our "yes" will have entailed losing many possible goods.

Because of the complexities involved in taking responsibility for the purposiveness of human life -- whether we interpret it as I do in terms of stewardship toward God, or as more humanistic Whiteheadians do in terms of the wisest possible care for the earth -- we cannot, I think, make our choices either mechanically or coolly, and need never call on ourselves or others to "defend" the choice made. Rather, I believe decisions about pregnancies -- to bear or to abort -- should be followed by celebration of the good realized and foreseen, by work to bring this good to birth, and by grief over the death of all the possibilities recognized as lost.

A second interpretation reintroduces the double sense of my own life on which I reflected at the outset: the oscilla- between questing and being called, between uncertainty and clarity. I find most faithful to my experience an image of the course of human life which is a movement from vagueness of inheritance and potentiality, toward identity and agency. I define identity as growing specificity and clarity of immediate presentness and self-reflective awareness. I define agency, here, as competence to act in relation to aims. Throughout this movement the aim pursued may or may not be achieved, may be achieved in part, or may be achieved with distortions. Whatever the conclusion, the result of my action contributes to my own future and to the lives of others. My self is thus a "becoming in response to my world," and the world, in turn, changes as my actions join with others' in constituting it.

My view contrasts with a more classical alternative. In its several forms, an identity called "soul" has sometimes been understood to be created whole and placed in a body at some time during gestations or at birth. Or, some have understood the soul to be created along with the body. In either case, however, it has been understood to remain unchanging throughout the changes of life. In contrast with the soul, historical and bodily changes then appear relatively ephemeral, without final significance. In that view, the task of the soul is to remain pure and whole in the face of threats and temptations; to do so it must defend against incursions from its own body and the surrounding environment.

In contrast to this rather static approach to the soul, I see human life as a movement toward a more specific identity and more responsible agency. My life, as any human life, involves risks every moment. My aim may be attained partially or distortedly, and in attaining certain goods inevitably I will also participate in loss, evil, or directly destructive actions. Even the normal processes of maturation entail necessary losses; growth to adulthood requires the loss of the child. When we speak of valuing personal integration,

rather than merely personal change, we are recognizing the
value of bearing our own child-selves along into our own
adulthood, transformed, but not destroyed. And yet, goods are
always lost in this process. Cultural rites of passage recognize both this giving up of the past, and the putting on
of the future.

During this movement through the course of one's life,
each phase is valuable both in its own right and for what it
offers to its future and to the world. Furthermore, God
values every human life at all points of its life-path. While
none of us is likely to achieve fully either our proximate
aims or the optimal hope God holds out for each human person,
our failures to achieve are not totally meaningless, nor are
they "the last word" for us. God is resourceful beyond human
agency, and whatever the state of the completed lives we
finally "offer to God," divine imagination and resourceful-
ness can be depended upon to transform them for participation
in larger harmonies and meanings.

Affirming this, I cannot regard the loss of life, no
matter how tragic, as hopeless or meaningless any more than
I can regard it as irrelevant. Every potentiality actualized
in a human life, at whatever level, is received into the life
of God, "saved," and made available for further objective effectiveness in the world. This applies to the aborted fetus
no less than to the deaths of persons at various points after
birth. Tragic as the loss of a fetus is, no fetus dies without hope of contribution.

The third interpretation that helps move from ambiguities
to some certainties concerns the "structure of existence."
This somewhat obscure phrase refers to the complex of potentials each human being shares simply by being human. In every
human life specific genetic inheritance and historical experience qualifies this set of possibilities in ways that make
each of us unique individuals. But all of us share this set

of possibilities. Its key may be called a "pattern for relationship," along the lines of Daniel Day Williams' description that the "image of God" in humanity is a "will to communion." We may also say the pattern is one of self-transcendence
self-hood in an animal body and in community with other human
lives and with the whole realm of creatures.[15] We are made
for each other, and for the world.

This structure has two main implications for pregnancy.
First, no human life fully actualizes or exhausts the possibilities of this pattern. Certain powerful lives suggest
some may actualize it optimally for themselves, yet as a
structure of potentials it remains objectively "eternal" with
capacities for further realization. A capacity for self-
transcending self-hood always remains not yet actualized.

Second, there is no point on the path of any particular
human life when one "attains to the structure;" it is not
strictly possible to say that one "has now become a human being." The structure is eternal, and as human lives generate
new human life, which moves along a continuum from fertilized
egg toward death, the structure attains to greater actualization and has increasing likelihood of rich enjoyment of its
being. Unity of body and soul exists throughout the continuum.
While it would perhaps be "neater" for a pro-choice position
if I could say that until such and such a time we are not
dealing with a really human life, I cannot see it this way.
At the same time, the more the structure is actualized, even
in utero, the more human it is. After birth, when truly social relationships are possible, the infant is "more human"
in as much as the sociality which major value in defining
human existence -- through human community -- is now for the
first time actualized as part of its being. These observations reflect the metaphysical basis for such common sense
statements as: a newborn baby "looks more human" than a 6-
week fetus. The more actualization has occurred, the more

the fetus seems human to us. We may recognize this phenomenon without giving ontological status to the different stages
in fetal development.

These preceding three interpretations do not lead directly to conclusions but rather cut both ways in the current
debate about pregnancy and abortion. In community, to speak
of the *purpose* of human life as stewardship of creation may
argue for or against bearing any particular fetus to birth.
The decision in any particular pregnancy involves antici-
pating all futures, the alternatives, and making moral not
merely utilitarian judgments. Which alternative tends toward
better stewardship of all the factors? Such a decision is
affected by appreciation for the value of all the human lives
intimately connected to the decision, for the value of each
contributor's freedom of choice, for the responsibility the
woman and the society bear on behalf of the fetus, and for
the value of the community's interests. Again, to speak of
the *course* of human life as growth toward specificity and
concrete achievement of aim might argue for placing higher
valuation on the lives in which the aims are more nearly
achieved than on those with mere potential. Then the claims
of the woman might preempt those of the fetus. But this is
not always the case. For some human purposes fragments of
achievement are as valuable as completed aims; an artist's
sketches may be prized as highly as her completed paintings.
In a sketch one may see not only where the idea tends, but
also recognize the abstract structure by which its envisager
hoped to move it forward. In some decisions, the fetus' potential may take priority over the woman's actualized achievements; in some it may not. Finally, interpreting the *structure* of human existence, one's essential humanity, as potentiality or pattern for relationship, does not argue simply
for any party's interests. The structure of human existence
demands integrated coordination of the claims of body, self-
transcendent selfhood, and community with other selves.

The first question I raised was: what is involved mor--
ally in the act of deciding what to do about a pregnancy? My
response: each decision bears moral components calling for
grief, celebration, and humility. "Grief" in any act of deciding involves saying "no" as well as "yes." Loss of some
sort characterizes both birth and abortion. This may appropriately be grieved. Furthermore, any decision involves human freedom; it is not merely weighing obligations but also
freely choosing to create one future rather than another.
This openness to a particular future may appropriately be
celebrated. Third, any deciding involves merely approximate
judging in the midst of the conflicting values of diverse human interests, appropriately leading the decider to humility.

Throughout these interpretations I have been concerned
to preserve appreciation of the woman's responsibility. In
this connection, it is relevant to recognize that one dimension of responsibility-taking is bearing guilt for losses on
one's decision has engendered. Guilt, an unavoidable conse-
quence of the freedom which is a precondition for responsibility. This recognition is important. A woman who feels
guilt after deciding to abort or after bearing a child is not
adequately heard if we attribute all her guilt to neurosis or
head-trips laid on her by sexist culture, or to the patriarchy
she has internalized. To feel such guilt is, at least partly,
to identify herself as a responsible person whose actions
matter and who realizes that every gain entails loss.

At the same time, not all the responsibility for the decision to bear or to abort is the woman's and not all the
guilt should be hers either. The whole society and especially each of its members who directly touch the woman's life
are factors inevitably considered in her moral decision.
Whatever in our attitudes and socio-economic systems supports
her decision, or makes one alternative seem the only option,
shares the guilt of the good lost because of the action not
chosen. All of us share complicity with women who decide to

have children they cannot care for adequately, who decide to
have abortions, who resist having any children at all, who
have children and abuse them, or who have children and live
out their lives in bondage to their fecundity. We share
their responsibility and their guilt.

My second question was: what is involved ethically in
the question whether abortion ought or ought not to be legal?
Although I would suggest that everything human is involved,
the "ought" is more clearly defined here than in the first
question. It may be derived from the interpretation of freedom I offered previously. If responsibility is to be taken,
free choice must be offered. All levels of the law should
support a woman's freedom in principle to make this choice.
At the same time, this introduces the need for institutional
coordination, which is related to the notion of collective
responsibility alluded to above. Doctors and medical staff
members have a freedom to choose which sometimes conflicts
with that of a woman whose choice concerning pregnancy differs from their own. Their freedom need not in principle be
denied by coercing them to perform surgery they choose not to
perform. Social changes should increasingly recognize the
possibility of conscientious objection to abortion, as well
as to war, and not penalize persons for holding this view.

V

An abortion is in the deepest sense an event fraught with
tragedy. Because it involves losing a complete set of potentials for individual human existence, the resultant loss to
the potential child and to society from an abortion must usually be assumed to be at least as grave as the benefits of
abortion to the mother and to society are wholesome, no matter what those benefits are. Yet, this recognition does not

change the fact that the decision concerning pregnancy always
involves genuinely conflicting values. None alone defines
human meaning -- not the right to life of the fetus, not the
right of the woman to particular gains she fears maternity
threatens, and not the community's rights to "productivity"
on the part of its citizens. None of these is absolute.

Amidst the relativities of these factors, the freedom
to decide responsibly must be both legally preserved and culturally encouraged; without authentic freedom choice becomes
indistinguishable from environmental coercion.

I recognize that evil lies on all hands, and that anyone
who decides about her pregnancy -- by virtue of claiming responsibility -- must be willing in principle to accept judgment more encompassing than her own. The deeper theological
issue does not, however, lie in determining what the judgment
of God might be. Given the tragic dimensions of any decision,
one may recognize that whichever alternative one chooses, the
choice will help create a future in which not only achievement but suffering, pain, and loss are components.

In the face of this suffering -- particularly that involved in the decision-making itself -- comfort, support, and
hope of healing are finally more important responses to offer
the woman than utilitarian or moral judgments about outcomes.
The pregnant woman faces the humbling recognition that she
cannot know in advance whether the greater evil lies in
aborting the fetus or in aborting her own previous anticipations and plans; nor can she know whether the greater good
lies in giving birth and raising her child, in giving birth
and placing the infant for adoption, or in aborting the fetus
and continuing to develop her vocation as say, a dancer. She
knows she cannot obtain all the relevant "information," since
much of it lies in the future, nor can she fully trust her
judgment. Her interests tempt her; tradition tempts her; her
friends tempt her; her self-doubts tempt her; her arrogance

and humbleness both tempt her. She is forced to make decisions in the face of motives she knows to be mixed, in hope
of a future she cannot foresee because she is creating it in
the very decision she is making. Her freedom to decide is a
terrible freedom.

It is important for her to recognize, therefore, that
her decisions are made in a world in which there is a call to
do the good, a call to be generous, a call to self-fulfill-
ment. But it is also a world in which it is also certain
that creation both recovers from wrong decisions and continues
to be alive to the processes of creation. It is important
for her to be open to the possibility that the way this all
"works" is not best understood by natural law, but by forgiveness.

If so, she may come to deeper awareness of herself as a
person legitimately questing and being called. What she
chooses and what she accepts are matters for which she takes
responsibility. Because she is free she may listen to the
many calls making claims upon her: from the fetus, from society, from systems of morality and law. She may also listen
to the voices within herself, urging her to continue her own
self-creating quest. She need not shut out any but may listen with care to each. Because she is in community she may
recognize that her ultimate decision is for others as well as
for herself, and that the specific character of that community
and what it offers her and the potential child must be considered. Most important, she may recognize that the presence
of God in the world as purposer and saver is a resource for
her decision-making, not -- as has too often been portrayed
to women -- primarily as moral arbiter, judge, and one-to-be-
placated. In this perspective, she may recognize that God's
purposes include her freedom to choose, and that God's resources of imagination and forgiveness are available to heal,
direct, and enrich her life whatever she decides. Her life

may be lived responsibly and creatively with or without a
pregnancy to complete and the gains and losses involved,
though real, are not the last word on anything.

The one who would counsel a woman in this decision-
making process may be most helpful if she or he acts on the
basis of the nature of human becoming sketched here. The
woman's freedom and responsibility may be recognized and supported by a counselor who encourages her with time and calm-
ness to listen to the many voices appealing for her attention. The better informed, the more aware of alternative
courses of action, and the more sensitive a woman is to the
richness and complexity of the decision she is making, the
more free she is to be responsible.

More subtle is the counselor's responsibility to avoid
leading the woman in the direction of the counselor's own
opinion. Supporting a woman's humanity, freedom, and respon-
sibility-in-community means being open to her choice, even
what it looks "wrong" to the counselor. Indeed, I suspect
that (1) the counselor's willingness to hear, to give cre-
dence to, to take as valuable the thinking-through of a per-
plexed, pained, decision-making woman, and (2) the sheer fact
that she is making a decision are probably more supportive
and clarifying of the woman's freedom and growing ability to
take responsibility than any explicit statements of support
a counselor might offer.

Both the woman and the counselor may be aided in the
decision-making process by recalling that each act, throughout the whole interrelated fabric of reality is self- and
world-creating. Through it, the new emerges by accepting the
offerings of its past, judging them, integrating them in reference to its own subjective purpose, and -- in turn -- of-
fering a new creation to the future for further contributions
to other actions.

In this process actions may be said to "forgive." They
creatively transform the inheritances of the past, whether

burdensome or blessed, into new aims for new futures. The
tragic action of aborting a fetus, with its specific evil,
is not an exception to the process of forgiveness, and even
the tragedy in this action may be redeemed in the subsequent
actions of the world.

NOTES

[1]Alfred North Whitehead, *Process and Reality,* corrected
edition, ed. David Ray Griffin, Donald W. Sherburne (New York:
Free Press, 1978) 351.

[2]Betty Sarvis and Hyman Rodman in their *The Abortion
Controversy* (New York: Columbia University Press, 1974) describe the contrast in this way. I prefer -- for reasons
that become obvious -- to describe the positions as "anti-
abortion" and "pro-choice," though I think both obscure the
complexity of the issues.

[3]*Beyond God the Father, Toward a Philosophy of Women's
Liberation* (Boston: Beacon Press, 1973) and *Gyn/Ecology, The
Meta-Ethics of Radical Feminism* (Boston: Beacon Press, 1978).

[4]The abstract bases for the discussion in this section
are found in Whitehead's *Process and Reality.* For the begin-
ner in Whiteheadian thought, I would suggest his *Modes of
Thought* as a starting point for the reader with some philosophical background or interest. For one who begins from a
base in Christian theology or an interest in the dynamics of
voluntary institutions (like the church), I suggest Norman
Pittenger's *The Christian Church as Social Process*
(Philadelphia: Westminister Press, 1971).

[5]*Process and Reality,* 18, 20.

[6]*Ibid.,* 43.

[7]*Ibid.,* 34f. According to Whitehead, personal order is
not limited to human beings; this is why the word "person" is
sticky in process thought, and why the abortion issue is not
particularly illuminated -- within a Whiteheadian perspective -- by the question: when does the fetus become "a

person." It is always a person, by Whitehead's criteria, but so is a tree, so the distinction is not helpful.

[8] *Ibid.,* 88.

[9] *Theology and Pastoral Care* (Philadelphia: Fortress Press, 1977).

[10] *Process and Reality,* 19.

[11] *Ibid.,* 22.

[12] These occur in *Adventures of Ideas* (New York: The Macmillan Company, 1933) and *The Aims of Education* (New York: The Macmillan Company, 1929).

[13] *The Spirit and the Forms of Love* (New York: Harper and Row, 1967), 134, 136.

[14] *Process and Reality,* 96.

[15] In emphasizing the animal body and human sociality, my view differs from that of John B. Cobb in *Theology and Pastoral Care,* where he emphasizes self-reflection and transcendence almost to the exclusion of other dimensions.

CONTRIBUTORS

SHEILA GREEVE DAVANEY received her doctoral degree from Harvard University. She has been a Research/Resource Associate in Women's Studies at Harvard Divinity School and is presently Assistant Professor of Theology at The Iliff School of Theology.

VALERIE C. SAIVING received her doctoral degree from the University of Chicago in 1963. She is presently Professor of Religious Studies at Hobart and William Smith Colleges and is the author of articles on female experience and religion.

JOHN B. COBB, JR. completed his doctoral work at the University of Chicago and is presently Ingraham Profesor of Theology at the School of Theology at Claremont, Avery Professor in the Claremont Graduate School and Director of the Center for Process Studies at Claremont. He is the author of many books and articles on process theology, including the recent *Christ in a Pluralistic Age*.

MARJORIE SUCHOCKI completed her graduate studies at Claremont Graduate School and is presently teaching at Pittsburgh Theological Seminary. She is the author of articles on feminism, process thought and Christian theology.

PENELOPE WASHBOURN completed her graduate work at Union Theological Seminary and has taught philosophy of religion and courses on women and religion at the College of Wooster, the University of Manitoba, and the Graduate Theological Union. She is the author of *Becoming Woman* and editor of *Seasons of Woman*.

JEAN LAMBERT has studied at Union Theological Seminary. She is presently Assistant Professor of Theology at St. Paul School of Theology.